S. Prt. 115–4

Congressional Pictorial Directory

2018

I0042214

UNITED STATES
GOVERNMENT PUBLISHING OFFICE
WASHINGTON: 2018

Compiled Under the Direction
of the
Joint Committee on Printing

Richard Shelby, Chairman

Contents

Closing date for compilation of the Pictorial Directory was February 1, 2018.

  * *House terms not consecutive.*
 †† *Four-year term, elected 2016.*

Contents

Donald J. Trump
President of the United States

Michael R. Pence
Vice President of the United States
and President of the Senate

SEAL OF THE SPEAKER
1789
UNITED STATES HOUSE OF REPRESENTATIVES

Paul D. Ryan
Speaker of the House of Representatives

Orrin G. Hatch
President pro tempore of the Senate

SENATE LEADERSHIP

Mitch McConnell
Majority Leader

Charles E. Schumer
Democratic Leader

John Cornyn
Majority Whip

Richard J. Durbin
Assistant Democratic Leader

HOUSE LEADERSHIP

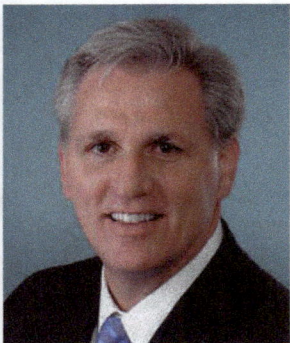

Kevin McCarthy
Majority Leader

Nancy Pelosi
Democratic Leader

Steve Scalise
Majority Whip

Steny H. Hoyer
Democratic Whip

SENATE OFFICERS AND OFFICIALS

Michael R. Pence
*Vice President of the United
States and President of the
Senate*

Orrin G. Hatch
*President pro tempore of the
Senate*

SENATE OFFICERS AND OFFICIALS

Julie E. Adams
Secretary

Frank J. Larkin
Sergeant at Arms

Laura C. Dove
Secretary of the Majority

Gary B. Myrick
Secretary of the Minority

SENATE OFFICERS AND OFFICIALS

Dr. Barry C. Black
Chaplain

Elizabeth MacDonough
Parliamentarian

HOUSE OFFICERS AND OFFICIALS

Paul D. Ryan
Speaker of the House of Representatives

Karen Haas
Clerk

Paul Irving
Sergeant at Arms

Philip G. Kiko
Chief Administrative Officer

HOUSE OFFICERS AND OFFICIALS

Patrick J. Conroy
Chaplain

Thomas J. Wickham, Jr.
Parliamentarian

Michael T. Ptasienski
Inspector General

CAPITOL OFFICIALS

Stephen T. Ayers
Architect of the Capitol

Dr. Brian Monahan
Attending Physician

Sen. Richard C. Shelby
of Tuscaloosa
Republican—Jan. 3, 1987

Sen. Doug Jones
of Fairfield
Democrat—Jan. 3, 2018

Rep. Bradley Byrne
of Fairhope (1st District)
Republican—3rd term

Rep. Martha Roby
of Montgomery (2nd District)
Republican—4th term

ALABAMA

Rep. Mike Rogers
of Anniston (3rd District)
Republican—8th term

Rep. Robert B. Aderholt
of Haleyville (4th District)
Republican—11th term

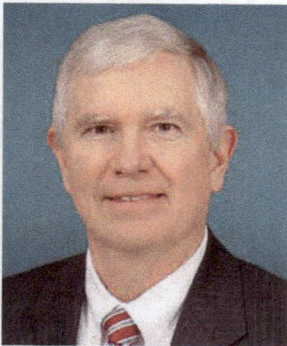

Rep. Mo Brooks
of Huntsville (5th District)
Republican—4th term

Rep. Gary J. Palmer
of Hoover (6th District)
Republican—2nd term

Rep. Terri A. Sewell
of Birmingham (7th District)
Democrat—4th term

ALASKA

Sen. Lisa Murkowski
of Girdwood
Republican—Jan. 7, 2003

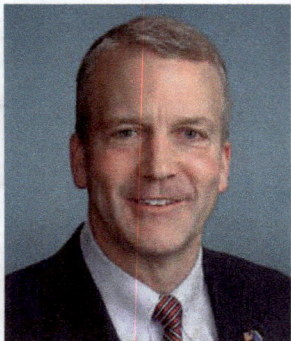

Sen. Dan Sullivan
of Anchorage
Republican—Jan. 6, 2015

Rep. Don Young
of Fort Yukon (At Large)
Republican—23rd term

Sen. John McCain
of Phoenix
Republican—Jan. 3, 1987

Sen. Jeff Flake
of Mesa
Republican—Jan. 3, 2013

Rep. Tom O'Halleran
of Sedona (1st District)
Democrat—1st term

Rep. Martha McSally
of Tucson (2nd District)
Republican—2nd term

ARIZONA

Rep. Raúl M. Grijalva
of Tucson (3rd District)
Democrat—8th term

Rep. Paul A. Gosar
of Prescott (4th District)
Republican—4th term

Rep. Andy Biggs
of Gilbert (5th District)
Republican—1st term

Rep. David Schweikert
of Fountain Hills (6th District)
Republican—4th term

Rep. Ruben Gallego
of Phoenix (7th District)
Democrat—2nd term

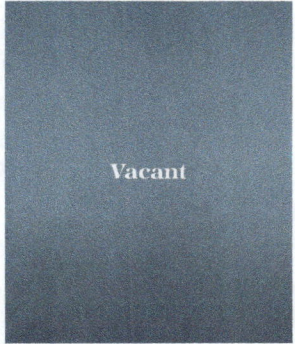

Vacant
(8th District)

Rep. Kyrsten Sinema
of Phoenix (9th District)
Democrat—3rd term

ARKANSAS

Sen. John Boozman
of Rogers
Republican—Jan. 5, 2011

Sen. Tom Cotton
of Dardanelle
Republican—Jan. 6, 2015

Rep. Eric A. "Rick" Crawford
of Jonesboro (1st District)
Republican—4th term

Rep. J. French Hill
of Little Rock (2nd District)
Republican—2nd term

Rep. Steve Womack
of Rogers (3rd District)
Republican—4th term

Rep. Bruce Westerman
of Hot Springs (4th District)
Republican—2nd term

CALIFORNIA

Sen. Dianne Feinstein
of San Francisco
Democrat—Nov. 10, 1992

Sen. Kamala D. Harris
of Oakland
Democrat—Jan. 3, 2017

Rep. Doug LaMalfa
of Oroville (1st District)
Republican—3rd term

Rep. Jared Huffman
of San Rafael (2nd District)
Democrat—3rd term

Rep. John Garamendi
of Walnut Grove (3rd District)
Democrat—5th term

Rep. Tom McClintock
of Roseville (4th District)
Republican—5th term

Rep. Mike Thompson
of St. Helena (5th District)
Democrat—10th term

Rep. Doris O. Matsui
of Sacramento (6th District)
Democrat—7th term

CALIFORNIA

Rep. Ami Bera
of Elk Grove (7th District)
Democrat—3rd term

Rep. Paul Cook
of Yucca Valley (8th District)
Republican—3rd term

Rep. Jerry McNerney
of Stockton (9th District)
Democrat—6th term

Rep. Jeff Denham
of Turlock (10th District)
Republican—4th term

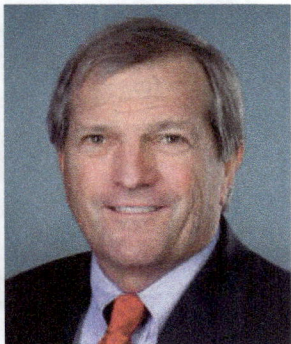

Rep. Mark DeSaulnier
of Concord (11th District)
Democrat—2nd term

Rep. Nancy Pelosi
of San Francisco (12th District)
Democrat—16th term

Rep. Barbara Lee
of Oakland (13th District)
Democrat—11th term

Rep. Jackie Speier
of Hillsborough (14th District)
Democrat—6th term

CALIFORNIA

Rep. Eric Swalwell
of Pleasanton (15th District)
Democrat—3rd term

Rep. Jim Costa
of Fresno (16th District)
Democrat—7th term

Rep. Ro Khanna
of Fremont (17th District)
Democrat—1st term

Rep. Anna G. Eshoo
of Atherton (18th District)
Democrat—13th term

Rep. Zoe Lofgren
of San José (19th District)
Democrat—12th term

Rep. Jimmy Panetta
of Carmel Valley (20th District)
Democrat—1st term

Rep. David G. Valadao
of Hanford (21st District)
Republican—3rd term

Rep. Devin Nunes
of Tulare (22nd District)
Republican—8th term

CALIFORNIA

Rep. Kevin McCarthy
of Bakersfield (23rd District)
Republican—6th term

Rep. Salud O. Carbajal
*of Santa Barbara
(24th District)*
Democrat—1st term

Rep. Stephen Knight
of Palmdale (25th District)
Republican—2nd term

Rep. Julia Brownley
*of Westlake Village
(26th District)*
Democrat—3rd term

Rep. Judy Chu
of Monterey Park (27th District)
Democrat—5th term

Rep. Adam B. Schiff
of Burbank (28th District)
Democrat—9th term

Rep. Tony Cárdenas
of Pacoima (29th District)
Democrat—3rd term

Rep. Brad Sherman
of Sherman Oaks
  (30th District)
Democrat—11th term

CALIFORNIA

Rep. Pete Aguilar
of Redlands (31st District)
Democrat—2nd term

Rep. Grace F. Napolitano
of Norwalk (32nd District)
Democrat—10th term

Rep. Ted Lieu
of Torrance (33rd District)
Democrat—2nd term

Rep. Jimmy Gomez
of Los Angeles (34th District)
Democrat—1st term

Rep. Norma J. Torres
of Pomona (35th District)
Democrat—2nd term

Rep. Raul Ruiz
of Coachella (36th District)
Democrat—3rd term

Rep. Karen Bass
of Los Angeles (37th District)
Democrat—4th term

Rep. Linda T. Sánchez
of Whittier (38th District)
Democrat—8th term

CALIFORNIA

Rep. Edward R. Royce
of Fullerton (39th District)
Republican—13th term

Rep. Lucille Roybal-Allard
of Downey (40th District)
Democrat—13th term

Rep. Mark Takano
of Riverside (41st District)
Democrat—3rd term

Rep. Ken Calvert
of Corona (42nd District)
Republican—13th term

Rep. Maxine Waters
of Los Angeles (43rd District)
Democrat—14th term

**Rep. Nanette Diaz
  Barragán**
of San Pedro (44th District)
Democrat—1st term

Rep. Mimi Walters
of Irvine (45th District)
Republican—2nd term

Rep. J. Luis Correa
of Santa Ana (46th District)
Democrat—1st term

CALIFORNIA

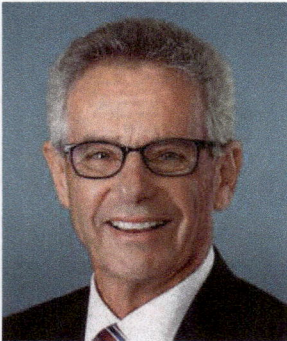

Rep. Alan S. Lowenthal
of Long Beach (47th District)
Democrat—3rd term

Rep. Dana Rohrabacher
of Costa Mesa (48th District)
Republican—15th term

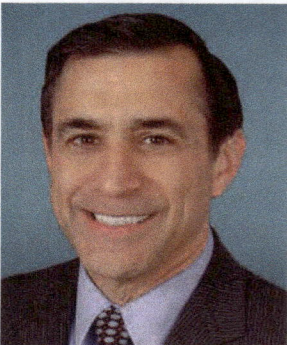

Rep. Darrell E. Issa
of Vista (49th District)
Republican—9th term

Rep. Duncan Hunter
of Alpine (50th District)
Republican—5th term

Rep. Juan Vargas
of San Diego (51st District)
Democrat—3rd term

Rep. Scott H. Peters
of San Diego (52nd District)
Democrat—3rd term

Rep. Susan A. Davis
of San Diego (53rd District)
Democrat—9th term

COLORADO

Sen. Michael F. Bennet
of Denver
Democrat—Jan. 22, 2009

Sen. Cory Gardner
of Yuma
Republican—Jan. 6, 2015

Rep. Diana DeGette
of Denver (1st District)
Democrat—11th term

Rep. Jared Polis
of Boulder (2nd District)
Democrat—5th term

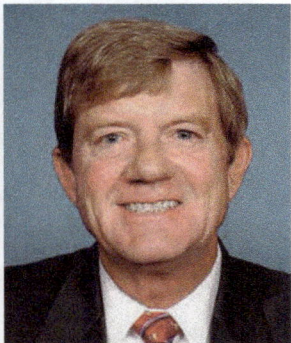

Rep. Scott R. Tipton
of Cortez (3rd District)
Republican—4th term

Rep. Ken Buck
of Windsor (4th District)
Republican—2nd term

Rep. Doug Lamborn
*of Colorado Springs
(5th District)*
Republican—6th term

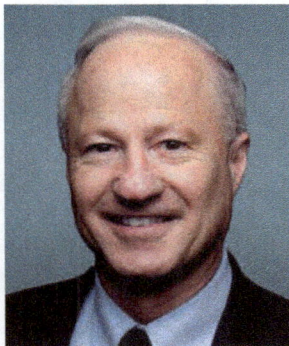

Rep. Mike Coffman
of Aurora (6th District)
Republican—5th term

COLORADO

Rep. Ed Perlmutter
of Golden (7th District)
Democrat—6th term

Sen. Richard Blumenthal
of Greenwich
Democrat—Jan. 5, 2011

**Sen. Christopher S.
Murphy**
of Cheshire
Democrat—Jan. 3, 2013

Rep. John B. Larson
of East Hartford (1st District)
Democrat—10th term

Rep. Joe Courtney
of Vernon (2nd District)
Democrat—6th term

CONNECTICUT

Rep. Rosa L. DeLauro
of New Haven (3rd District)
Democrat—14th term

Rep. James A. Himes
of Cos Cob (4th District)
Democrat—5th term

Rep. Elizabeth H. Esty
of Cheshire (5th District)
Democrat—3rd term

Sen. Thomas R. Carper
of Wilmington
Democrat—Jan. 3, 2001

Sen. Christopher A. Coons
of Wilmington
Democrat—Nov. 15, 2010

Rep. Lisa Blunt Rochester
of Wilmington (At Large)
Democrat—1st term

FLORIDA

Sen. Bill Nelson
of Orlando
Democrat—Jan. 3, 2001

Sen. Marco Rubio
of Miami
Republican—Jan. 5, 2011

Rep. Matt Gaetz
of Fort Walton Beach
(1st District)
Republican—1st term

Rep. Neal P. Dunn
of Panama City (2nd District)
Republican—1st term

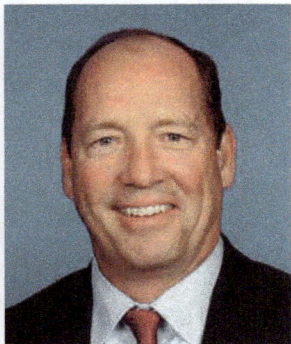

Rep. Ted S. Yoho
of Gainesville (3rd District)
Republican—3rd term

Rep. John H. Rutherford
of Jacksonville (4th District)
Republican—1st term

Rep. Al Lawson, Jr.
of Tallahassee (5th District)
Democrat—1st term

Rep. Ron DeSantis
of Palm Coast (6th District)
Republican—3rd term

FLORIDA

Rep. Stephanie N. Murphy
of Winter Park (7th District)
Democrat—1st term

Rep. Bill Posey
of Rockledge (8th District)
Republican—5th term

Rep. Darren Soto
of Kissimmee (9th District)
Democrat—1st term

Rep. Val Butler Demings
of Orlando (10th District)
Democrat—1st term

Rep. Daniel Webster
of Clermont (11th District)
Republican—4th term

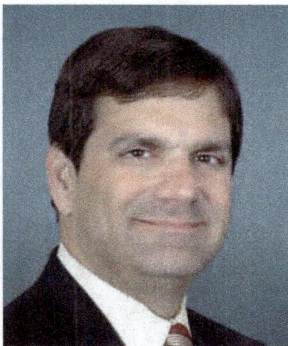

Rep. Gus M. Bilirakis
of Palm Harbor (12th District)
Republican—6th term

Rep. Charlie Crist
of St. Petersburg (13th District)
Democrat—1st term

Rep. Kathy Castor
of Tampa (14th District)
Democrat—6th term

FLORIDA

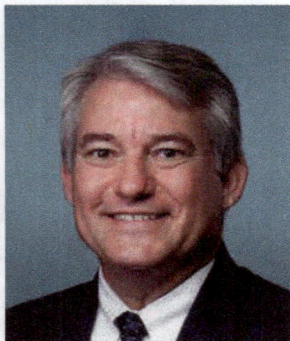

Rep. Dennis A. Ross
of Lakeland (15th District)
Republican—4th term

Rep. Vern Buchanan
of Sarasota (16th District)
Republican—6th term

Rep. Thomas J. Rooney
of Okeechobee (17th District)
Republican—5th term

Rep. Brian J. Mast
of Palm City (18th District)
Republican—1st term

Rep. Francis Rooney
of Naples (19th District)
Republican—1st term

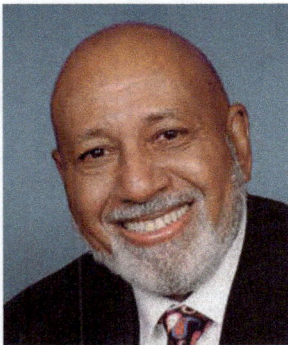

Rep. Alcee L. Hastings
of Delray Beach (20th District)
Democrat—13th term

Rep. Lois Frankel
*of West Palm Beach
(21st District)*
Democrat—3rd term

Rep. Theodore E. Deutch
of Boca Raton (22nd District)
Democrat—5th term

FLORIDA

Rep. Debbie Wasserman Schultz
of Weston (23rd District)
Democrat—7th term

Rep. Frederica S. Wilson
of Miami Gardens (24th District)
Democrat—4th term

Rep. Mario Diaz-Balart
of Miami (25th District)
Republican—8th term

Rep. Carlos Curbelo
of Miami (26th District)
Republican—2nd term

Rep. Ileana Ros-Lehtinen
of Miami (27th District)
Republican—15th term

GEORGIA

Sen. Johnny Isakson
of Marietta
Republican—Jan. 4, 2005

Sen. David Perdue
of Glynn County
Republican—Jan. 6, 2015

Rep. Earl L. "Buddy" Carter
of Pooler (1st District)
Republican—2nd term

Rep. Sanford D. Bishop, Jr.
of Albany (2nd District)
Democrat—13th term

Rep. A. Drew Ferguson IV
of West Point (3rd District)
Republican—1st term

Rep. Henry C. "Hank" Johnson, Jr.
of Lithonia (4th District)
Democrat—6th term

Rep. John Lewis
of Atlanta (5th District)
Democrat—16th term

Rep. Karen C. Handel
of Roswell (6th District)
Republican—1st term

GEORGIA

Rep. Rob Woodall
of Lawrenceville (7th District)
Republican—4th term

Rep. Austin Scott
of Tifton (8th District)
Republican—4th term

Rep. Doug Collins
of Gainesville (9th District)
Republican—3rd term

Rep. Jody B. Hice
of Monroe (10th District)
Republican—2nd term

Rep. Barry Loudermilk
of Cassville (11th District)
Republican—2nd term

Rep. Rick W. Allen
of Augusta (12th District)
Republican—2nd term

Rep. David Scott
of Atlanta (13th District)
Democrat—8th term

Rep. Tom Graves
of Ranger (14th District)
Republican—5th term

HAWAII

Sen. Brian E. Schatz
of Honolulu
Democrat—Dec. 27, 2012

Sen. Mazie K. Hirono
of Honolulu
Democrat—Jan. 3, 2013

Rep. Colleen Hanabusa
of Honolulu (1st District)
Democrat—4th term *

Rep. Tulsi Gabbard
of Kailua (2nd District)
Democrat—3rd term

Sen. Mike Crapo
of Idaho Falls
Republican—Jan. 6, 1999

Sen. James E. Risch
of Boise
Republican—Jan. 6, 2009

Rep. Raúl R. Labrador
of Eagle (1st District)
Republican—4th term

Rep. Michael K. Simpson
of Idaho Falls (2nd District)
Republican—10th term

ILLINOIS

Sen. Richard J. Durbin
of Springfield
Democrat—Jan. 7, 1997

Sen. Tammy Duckworth
of Hoffman Estates
Democrat—Jan. 3, 2017

Rep. Bobby L. Rush
of Chicago (1st District)
Democrat—13th term

Rep. Robin L. Kelly
of Matteson (2nd District)
Democrat—3rd term

Rep. Daniel Lipinski
*of Western Springs
(3rd District)*

Democrat—7th term

Rep. Luis V. Gutiérrez
of Chicago (4th District)

Democrat—13th term

Rep. Mike Quigley
of Chicago (5th District)

Democrat—5th term

Rep. Peter J. Roskam
of Wheaton (6th District)

Republican—6th term

ILLINOIS

Rep. Danny K. Davis
of Chicago (7th District)
Democrat—11th term

Rep. Raja Krishnamoorthi
of Schaumburg (8th District)
Democrat—1st term

Rep. Janice D. Schakowsky
of Evanston (9th District)
Democrat—10th term

Rep. Bradley Scott Schneider
of Deerfield (10th District)
Democrat—2nd term *

Rep. Bill Foster
of Naperville (11th District)
Democrat—5th term *

Rep. Mike Bost
of Murphysboro (12th District)
Republican—2nd term

Rep. Rodney Davis
of Taylorville (13th District)
Republican—3rd term

Rep. Randy Hultgren
of Plano (14th District)
Republican—4th term

ILLINOIS

Rep. John Shimkus
of Collinsville (15th District)
Republican—11th term

Rep. Adam Kinzinger
of Channahon (16th District)
Republican—4th term

Rep. Cheri Bustos
of Moline (17th District)
Democrat—3rd term

Rep. Darin LaHood
of Peoria (18th District)
Republican—2nd term

Sen. Joe Donnelly
of Granger
Democrat—Jan. 3, 2013

Sen. Todd Young
of Bloomington
Republican—Jan. 3, 2017

Rep. Peter J. Visclosky
of Merrillville (1st District)
Democrat—17th term

Rep. Jackie Walorski
of Elkhart (2nd District)
Republican—3rd term

INDIANA

Rep. Jim Banks
of Columbia City (3rd District)
Republican—1st term

Rep. Todd Rokita
of Brownsburg (4th District)
Republican—4th term

Rep. Susan W. Brooks
of Carmel (5th District)
Republican—3rd term

Rep. Luke Messer
of Greensburg (6th District)
Republican—3rd term

Rep. André Carson
of Indianapolis (7th District)
Democrat—6th term

Rep. Larry Bucshon
of Newburgh (8th District)
Republican—4th term

Rep. Trey Hollingsworth
of Jeffersonville (9th District)
Republican—1st term

IOWA

Sen. Chuck Grassley
of New Hartford
Republican—Jan. 3, 1981

Sen. Joni Ernst
of Red Oak
Republican—Jan. 6, 2015

Rep. Rod Blum
of Dubuque (1st District)
Republican—2nd term

Rep. David Loebsack
of Iowa City (2nd District)
Democrat—6th term

Rep. David Young
of Van Meter (3rd District)
Republican—2nd term

Rep. Steve King
of Kiron (4th District)
Republican—8th term

KANSAS

Sen. Pat Roberts
of Dodge City
Republican—Jan. 7, 1997

Sen. Jerry Moran
of Manhattan
Republican—Jan. 5, 2011

Rep. Roger W. Marshall
of Great Bend (1st District)
Republican—1st term

Rep. Lynn Jenkins
of Topeka (2nd District)
Republican—5th term

Rep. Kevin Yoder
of Overland Park (3rd District)
Republican—4th term

Rep. Ron Estes
of Wichita (4th District)
Republican—1st term

KENTUCKY

Sen. Mitch McConnell
of Louisville
Republican—Jan. 3, 1985

Sen. Rand Paul
of Bowling Green
Republican—Jan. 5, 2011

Rep. James Comer
of Tompkinsville (1st District)
Republican—2nd term

Rep. Brett Guthrie
of Bowling Green (2nd District)
Republican—5th term

Rep. John A. Yarmuth
of Louisville (3rd District)
Democrat—6th term

Rep. Thomas Massie
of Garrison (4th District)
Republican—4th term

Rep. Harold Rogers
of Somerset (5th District)
Republican—19th term

Rep. Andy Barr
of Lexington (6th District)
Republican—3rd term

LOUISIANA

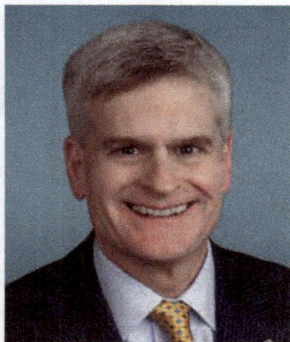

Sen. Bill Cassidy, M.D.
of Baton Rouge
Republican—Jan. 6, 2015

Sen. John Kennedy
of Madisonville
Republican—Jan. 3, 2017

Rep. Steve Scalise
of Jefferson (1st District)
Republican—6th term

Rep. Cedric L. Richmond
of New Orleans (2nd District)
Democrat—4th term

Rep. Clay Higgins
of Lafayette (3rd District)
Republican—1st term

Rep. Mike Johnson
of Benton (4th District)
Republican—1st term

Rep. Ralph Lee Abraham
of Alto (5th District)
Republican—2nd term

Rep. Garret Graves
of Baton Rouge (6th District)
Republican—2nd term

MAINE

Sen. Susan M. Collins
of Bangor
Republican—Jan. 7, 1997

Sen. Angus S. King, Jr.
of Brunswick
Independent—Jan. 3, 2013

Rep. Chellie Pingree
of North Haven (1st District)
Democrat—5th term

Rep. Bruce Poliquin
of Oakland (2nd District)
Republican—2nd term

Sen. Benjamin L. Cardin
of Baltimore
Democrat—Jan. 4, 2007

Sen. Chris Van Hollen
of Kensington
Democrat—Jan. 3, 2017

Rep. Andy Harris
of Cockeysville (1st District)
Republican—4th term

Rep. C.A. Dutch Ruppersberger
of Cockeysville (2nd District)
Democrat—8th term

MARYLAND

Rep. John P. Sarbanes
of Baltimore (3rd District)
Democrat—6th term

Rep. Anthony G. Brown
of Mitchellville (4th District)
Democrat—1st term

Rep. Steny H. Hoyer
of Mechanicsville (5th District)
Democrat—19th term

Rep. John K. Delaney
of Potomac (6th District)
Democrat—3rd term

Rep. Elijah E. Cummings
of Baltimore (7th District)
Democrat—12th term

Rep. Jamie Raskin
of Takoma Park (8th District)
Democrat—1st term

MASSACHUSETTS

Sen. Elizabeth Warren
of Cambridge
Democrat—Jan. 3, 2013

Sen. Edward J. Markey
of Malden
Democrat—Jul. 16, 2013

Rep. Richard E. Neal
of Springfield (1st District)
Democrat—15th term

Rep. James P. McGovern
of Worcester (2nd District)
Democrat—11th term

Rep. Niki Tsongas
of Lowell (3rd District)
Democrat—6th term

**Rep. Joseph P.
 Kennedy III**
of Newton (4th District)
Democrat—3rd term

Rep. Katherine M. Clark
of Melrose (5th District)
Democrat—3rd term

Rep. Seth Moulton
of Salem (6th District)
Democrat—2nd term

MASSACHUSETTS

Rep. Michael E. Capuano
of Somerville (7th District)
Democrat—10th term

Rep. Stephen F. Lynch
of South Boston (8th District)
Democrat—9th term

Rep. William R. Keating
of Bourne (9th District)
Democrat—4th term

Sen. Debbie Stabenow
of Lansing
Democrat—Jan. 3, 2001

Sen. Gary C. Peters
of Bloomfield Hills
Democrat—Jan. 6, 2015

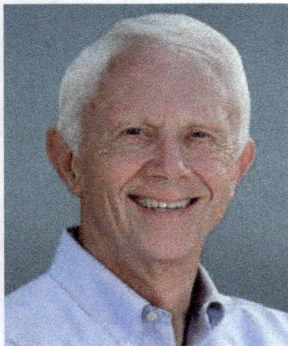

Rep. Jack Bergman
of Watersmeet (1st District)
Republican—1st term

Rep. Bill Huizenga
of Zeeland (2nd District)
Republican—4th term

MICHIGAN

Rep. Justin Amash
*of Cascade Township
(3rd District)*
Republican—4th term

Rep. John R. Moolenaar
of Midland (4th District)
Republican—2nd term

Rep. Daniel T. Kildee
of Flushing (5th District)
Democrat—3rd term

Rep. Fred Upton
of St. Joseph (6th District)
Republican—16th term

Rep. Tim Walberg
of Tipton (7th District)
Republican—5th term *

Rep. Mike Bishop
of Rochester (8th District)
Republican—2nd term

Rep. Sander M. Levin
of Royal Oak (9th District)
Democrat—18th term

Rep. Paul Mitchell
of Dryden (10th District)
Republican—1st term

MICHIGAN

Rep. David A. Trott
of Birmingham (11th District)
Republican—2nd term

Rep. Debbie Dingell
of Dearborn (12th District)
Democrat—2nd term

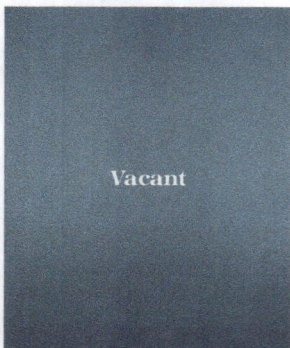

Vacant

Vacant
(13th District)

Rep. Brenda L. Lawrence
of Southfield (14th District)
Democrat—2nd term

Sen. Amy Klobuchar
of Minneapolis
Democrat—Jan. 4, 2007

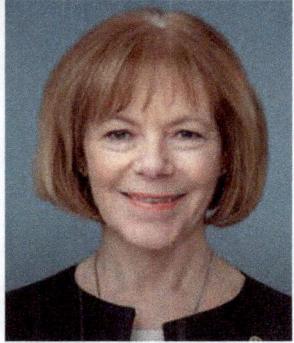

Sen. Tina Smith
of Minneapolis
Democrat—Jan. 3, 2018

Rep. Timothy J. Walz
of Mankato (1st District)
Democrat—6th term

Rep. Jason Lewis
of Woodbury (2nd District)
Republican—1st term

MINNESOTA

Rep. Erik Paulsen
of Eden Prairie (3rd District)
Republican—5th term

Rep. Betty McCollum
of St. Paul (4th District)
Democrat—9th term

Rep. Keith Ellison
of Minneapolis (5th District)
Democrat—6th term

Rep. Tom Emmer
of Delano (6th District)
Republican—2nd term

Rep. Collin C. Peterson
of Detroit Lakes (7th District)
Democrat—14th term

Rep. Richard M. Nolan
of Crosby (8th District)
Democrat—6th term *

MISSISSIPPI

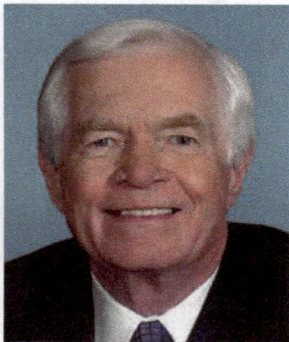

Sen. Thad Cochran
of Oxford
Republican—Dec. 27, 1978

Sen. Roger F. Wicker
of Tupelo
Republican—Jan. 22, 2008

Rep. Trent Kelly
of Saltillo (1st District)
Republican—2nd term

Rep. Bennie G. Thompson
of Bolton (2nd District)
Democrat—13th term

Rep. Gregg Harper
of Pearl (3rd District)
Republican—5th term

Rep. Steven M. Palazzo
of Biloxi (4th District)
Republican—4th term

MISSOURI

Sen. Claire McCaskill
of Kirkwood
Democrat—Jan. 4, 2007

Sen. Roy Blunt
of Springfield
Republican—Jan. 5, 2011

Rep. Wm. Lacy Clay
of St. Louis (1st District)
Democrat—9th term

Rep. Ann Wagner
of Ballwin (2nd District)
Republican—3rd term

Rep. Blaine Luetkemeyer
of St. Elizabeth (3rd District)
Republican—5th term

Rep. Vicky Hartzler
of Harrisonville (4th District)
Republican—4th term

Rep. Emanuel Cleaver
of Kansas City (5th District)
Democrat—7th term

Rep. Sam Graves
of Tarkio (6th District)
Republican—9th term

MISSOURI

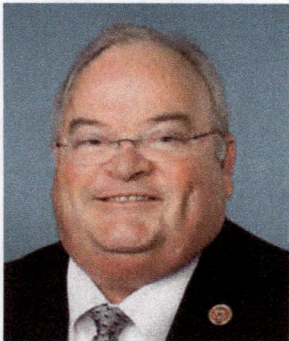

Rep. Billy Long
of Springfield (7th District)
Republican—4th term

Rep. Jason Smith
of Salem (8th District)
Republican—3rd term

Sen. Jon Tester
of Big Sandy
Democrat—Jan. 4, 2007

Sen. Steve Daines
of Bozeman
Republican—Jan. 6, 2015

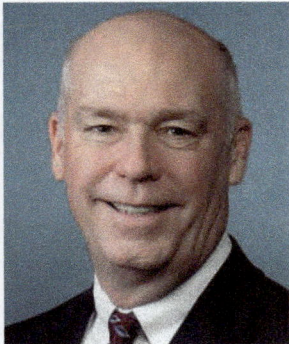

Rep. Greg Gianforte
of Bozeman (At Large)
Republican—1st term

NEBRASKA

Sen. Deb Fischer
of Valentine
Republican—Jan. 3, 2013

Sen. Ben Sasse
of Fremont
Republican—Jan. 6, 2015

Rep. Jeff Fortenberry
of Lincoln (1st District)
Republican—7th term

Rep. Don Bacon
of Papillion (2nd District)
Republican—1st term

Rep. Adrian Smith
of Gering (3rd District)
Republican—6th term

NEVADA

Sen. Dean Heller
of Carson City
Republican—May 9, 2011

Sen. Catherine Cortez Masto
of Las Vegas
Democrat—Jan. 3, 2017

Rep. Dina Titus
of Las Vegas (1st District)
Democrat—4th term *

Rep. Mark E. Amodei
of Carson City (2nd District)
Republican—4th term

Rep. Jacky Rosen
of Henderson (3rd District)
Democrat—1st term

Rep. Ruben J. Kihuen
of Las Vegas (4th District)
Democrat—1st term

NEW HAMPSHIRE

Sen. Jeanne Shaheen
of Madbury
Democrat—Jan. 6, 2009

Sen. Maggie Hassan
of Newfields
Democrat—Jan. 3, 2017

Rep. Carol Shea-Porter
of Rochester (1st District)
Democrat—4th term *

Rep. Ann M. Kuster
of Hopkinton (2nd District)
Democrat—3rd term

Sen. Robert Menendez
of North Bergen
Democrat—Jan. 18, 2006

Sen. Cory A. Booker
of Newark
Democrat—Oct. 31, 2013

Rep. Donald Norcross
of Camden City (1st District)
Democrat—3rd term

Rep. Frank A. LoBiondo
of Ventnor (2nd District)
Republican—12th term

Rep. Thomas MacArthur
of Toms River (3rd District)
Republican—2nd term

Rep. Christopher H. Smith
of Hamilton (4th District)
Republican—19th term

Rep. Josh Gottheimer
of Wyckoff (5th District)
Democrat—1st term

Rep. Frank Pallone, Jr.
of Long Branch (6th District)
Democrat—16th term

Rep. Leonard Lance
of Clinton Township
(7th District)
Republican—5th term

Rep. Albio Sires
of West New York
(8th District)
Democrat—7th term

Rep. Bill Pascrell, Jr.
of Paterson (9th District)
Democrat—11th term

**Rep. Donald M.
Payne, Jr.**
of Newark (10th District)
Democrat—4th term

NEW JERSEY

Rep. Rodney P. Frelinghuysen
of Morristown (11th District)
Republican—12th term

Rep. Bonnie Watson Coleman
of Ewing Township (12th District)
Democrat—2nd term

Sen. Tom Udall
of Santa Fe
Democrat—Jan. 6, 2009

Sen. Martin Heinrich
of Albuquerque
Democrat—Jan. 3, 2013

**Rep. Michelle
Lujan Grisham**
of Albuquerque (1st District)
Democrat—3rd term

Rep. Stevan Pearce
of Hobbs (2nd District)
Republican—7th term *

NEW MEXICO

Rep. Ben Ray Luján
of Nambé (3rd District)
Democrat—5th term

Sen. Charles E. Schumer
of Brooklyn
Democrat—Jan. 6, 1999

Sen. Kirsten Gillibrand
of Brunswick
Democrat—Jan. 27, 2009

Rep. Lee M. Zeldin
of Shirley (1st District)
Republican—2nd term

Rep. Peter T. King
of Seaford (2nd District)
Republican—13th term

NEW YORK

Rep. Thomas R. Suozzi
of Glen Cove (3rd District)
Democrat—1st term

Rep. Kathleen M. Rice
of Garden City (4th District)
Democrat—2nd term

Rep. Gregory W. Meeks
of Queens (5th District)
Democrat—11th term

Rep. Grace Meng
of Queens (6th District)
Democrat—3rd term

Rep. Nydia M. Velázquez
of Brooklyn (7th District)
Democrat—13th term

Rep. Hakeem S. Jeffries
of Brooklyn (8th District)
Democrat—3rd term

Rep. Yvette D. Clarke
of Brooklyn (9th District)
Democrat—6th term

Rep. Jerrold Nadler
of New York (10th District)
Democrat—14th term

NEW YORK

Rep. Daniel M. Donovan, Jr.
of Staten Island (11th District)
Republican—2nd term

Rep. Carolyn B. Maloney
of New York (12th District)
Democrat—13th term

Rep. Adriano Espaillat
of New York (13th District)
Democrat—1st term

Rep. Joseph Crowley
of Queens/Bronx (14th District)
Democrat—10th term

Rep. José E. Serrano
of Bronx (15th District)
Democrat—15th term

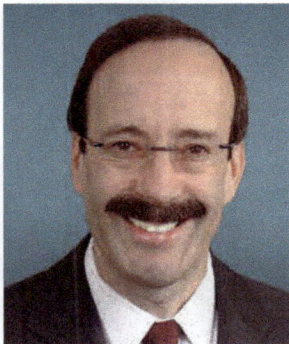

Rep. Eliot L. Engel
of Bronx (16th District)
Democrat—15th term

Rep. Nita M. Lowey
of Harrison (17th District)
Democrat—15th term

Rep. Sean Patrick Maloney
of Cold Spring (18th District)
Democrat—3rd term

NEW YORK

Rep. John J. Faso
of Kinderhook (19th District)
Republican—1st term

Rep. Paul Tonko
of Amsterdam (20th District)
Democrat—5th term

Rep. Elise M. Stefanik
of Willsboro (21st District)
Republican—2nd term

Rep. Claudia Tenney
*of New Hartford
(22nd District)*
Republican—1st term

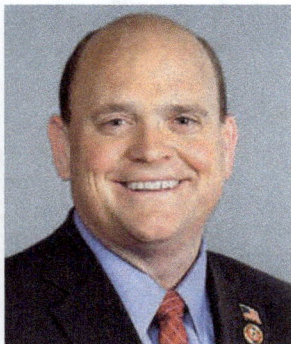

Rep. Tom Reed
of Corning (23rd District)
Republican—5th term

Rep. John Katko
of Syracuse (24th District)
Republican—2nd term

**Rep. Louise McIntosh
  Slaughter**
of Fairport (25th District)
Democrat—16th term

Rep. Brian Higgins
of Buffalo (26th District)
Democrat—7th term

NEW YORK

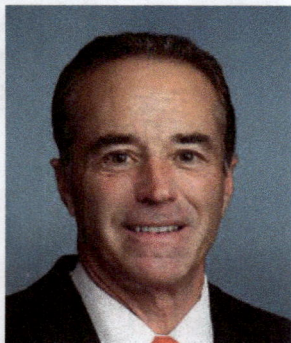

Rep. Chris Collins
of Clarence (27th District)
Republican—3rd term

Sen. Richard Burr
of Winston-Salem
Republican—Jan. 4, 2005

Sen. Thom Tillis
of Huntersville
Republican—Jan. 6, 2015

Rep. G.K. Butterfield
of Wilson (1st District)
Democrat—8th term

Rep. George Holding
of Raleigh (2nd District)
Republican—3rd term

NORTH CAROLINA

Rep. Walter B. Jones
of Farmville (3rd District)
Republican—12th term

Rep. David E. Price
of Chapel Hill (4th District)
Democrat—15th term *

Rep. Virginia Foxx
of Banner Elk (5th District)
Republican—7th term

Rep. Mark Walker
of Greensboro (6th District)
Republican—2nd term

Rep. David Rouzer
of McGee's Crossroad
(7th District)
Republican—2nd term

Rep. Richard Hudson
of Concord (8th District)
Republican—3rd term

Rep. Robert Pittenger
of Charlotte (9th District)
Republican—3rd term

Rep. Patrick T. McHenry
of Lake Norman (10th District)
Republican—7th term

NORTH CAROLINA

Rep. Mark Meadows
of Skyland (11th District)
Republican—3rd term

Rep. Alma S. Adams
of Charlotte (12th District)
Democrat—3rd term

Rep. Ted Budd
of Advance (13th District)
Republican—1st term

Sen. John Hoeven
of Bismarck
Republican—Jan. 5, 2011

Sen. Heidi Heitkamp
of Mantador
Democrat—Jan. 3, 2013

Rep. Kevin Cramer
of Bismarck (At Large)
Republican—3rd term

Sen. Sherrod Brown
of Cleveland
Democrat—Jan. 4, 2007

Sen. Rob Portman
of Terrace Park
Republican—Jan. 5, 2011

Rep. Steve Chabot
of Cincinnati (1st District)
Republican—11th term *

Rep. Brad R. Wenstrup
of Cincinnati (2nd District)
Republican—3rd term

Rep. Joyce Beatty
of Columbus (3rd District)
Democrat—3rd term

Rep. Jim Jordan
of Urbana (4th District)
Republican—6th term

Rep. Robert E. Latta
of Bowling Green (5th District)
Republican—6th term

Rep. Bill Johnson
of Marietta (6th District)
Republican—4th term

OHIO

Rep. Bob Gibbs
of Lakeville (7th District)
Republican—4th term

Rep. Warren Davidson
of Troy (8th District)
Republican—2nd term

Rep. Marcy Kaptur
of Toledo (9th District)
Democrat—18th term

Rep. Michael R. Turner
of Dayton (10th District)
Republican—8th term

Rep. Marcia L. Fudge
of Warrensville Heights
(11th District)
Democrat—6th term

Vacant
(12th District)

Rep. Tim Ryan
of Warren (13th District)
Democrat—8th term

Rep. David P. Joyce
of Russell Township
(14th District)
Republican—3rd term

OHIO

Rep. Steve Stivers
of Columbus (15th District)
Republican—4th term

Rep. James B. Renacci
of Wadsworth (16th District)
Republican—4th term

Sen. James M. Inhofe
of Tulsa
Republican—Nov. 17, 1994

Sen. James Lankford
of Edmond
Republican—Jan. 6, 2015

Rep. Jim Bridenstine
of Tulsa (1st District)
Republican—3rd term

Rep. Markwayne Mullin
of Westville (2nd District)
Republican—3rd term

OKLAHOMA

Rep. Frank D. Lucas
of Cheyenne (3rd District)
Republican—13th term

Rep. Tom Cole
of Moore (4th District)
Republican—8th term

Rep. Steve Russell
of Oklahoma City (5th District)
Republican—2nd term

Sen. Ron Wyden
of Portland
Democrat—Feb. 6, 1996

Sen. Jeff Merkley
of East Portland
Democrat—Jan. 6, 2009

Rep. Suzanne Bonamici
of Washington County
(1st District)
Democrat—4th term

Rep. Greg Walden
of Hood River (2nd District)
Republican—10th term

OREGON

Rep. Earl Blumenauer
of Portland (3rd District)
Democrat—12th term

Rep. Peter A. DeFazio
of Springfield (4th District)
Democrat—16th term

Rep. Kurt Schrader
of Canby (5th District)
Democrat—5th term

Sen. Robert P. Casey, Jr.
of Scranton
Democrat—Jan. 4, 2007

Sen. Pat Toomey
of Zionsville
Republican—Jan. 5, 2011

Rep. Robert A. Brady
of Philadelphia (1st District)
Democrat—11th term

Rep. Dwight Evans
of Philadelphia (2nd District)
Democrat—2nd term

PENNSYLVANIA

Rep. Mike Kelly
of Butler (3rd District)
Republican—4th term

Rep. Scott Perry
of Dillsburg (4th District)
Republican—3rd term

Rep. Glenn Thompson
of Howard (5th District)
Republican—5th term

Rep. Ryan A. Costello
of West Chester (6th District)
Republican—2nd term

Rep. Patrick Meehan
of Chadds Ford (7th District)
Republican—4th term

Rep. Brian K. Fitzpatrick
of Levittown (8th District)
Republican—1st term

Rep. Bill Shuster
of Hollidaysburg (9th District)
Republican—9th term

Rep. Tom Marino
of Williamsport (10th District)
Republican—4th term

PENNSYLVANIA

Rep. Lou Barletta
of Hazleton (11th District)
Republican—4th term

Rep. Keith J. Rothfus
of Sewickley (12th District)
Republican—3rd term

Rep. Brendan F. Boyle
of Philadelphia (13th District)
Democrat—2nd term

Rep. Michael F. Doyle
of Pittsburgh (14th District)
Democrat—12th term

Rep. Charles W. Dent
of Allentown (15th District)
Republican—7th term

Rep. Lloyd Smucker
of Lancaster (16th District)
Republican—1st term

Rep. Matt Cartwright
of Moosic (17th District)
Democrat—3rd term

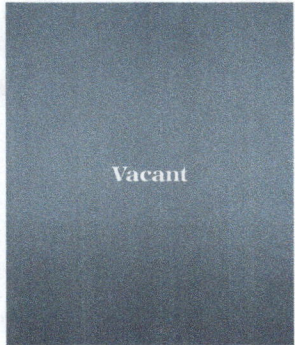

Vacant

Vacant
(18th District)

RHODE ISLAND

Sen. Jack Reed
of Jamestown
Democrat—Jan. 7, 1997

Sen. Sheldon Whitehouse
of Newport
Democrat—Jan. 4, 2007

Rep. David N. Cicilline
of Providence (1st District)
Democrat—4th term

Rep. James R. Langevin
of Warwick (2nd District)
Democrat—9th term

Sen. Lindsey Graham
of Seneca
Republican—Jan. 7, 2003

Sen. Tim Scott
of North Charleston
Republican—Jan. 3, 2013

Rep. Mark Sanford
of Charleston (1st District)
Republican—6th term *

Rep. Joe Wilson
of Springdale (2nd District)
Republican—9th term

SOUTH CAROLINA

Rep. Jeff Duncan
of Laurens (3rd District)
Republican—4th term

Rep. Trey Gowdy
of Spartanburg (4th District)
Republican—4th term

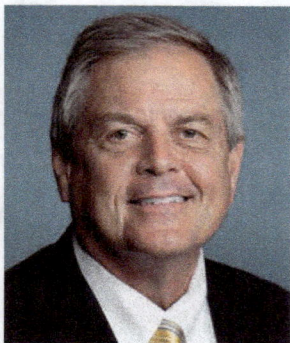

Rep. Ralph Norman
of Rock Hill (5th District)
Republican—1st term

Rep. James E. Clyburn
of Columbia (6th District)
Democrat—13th term

Rep. Tom Rice
of Myrtle Beach (7th District)
Republican—3rd term

SOUTH DAKOTA

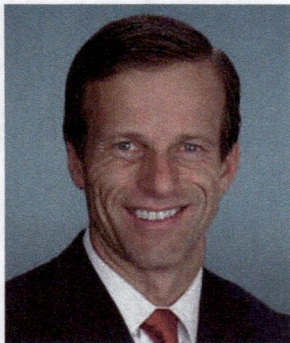

Sen. John Thune
of Murdo
Republican—Jan. 4, 2005

Sen. Mike Rounds
of Huron
Republican—Jan. 6, 2015

Rep. Kristi L. Noem
of Castlewood (At Large)
Republican—4th term

Sen. Lamar Alexander
of Maryville
Republican—Jan. 7, 2003

Sen. Bob Corker
of Chattanooga
Republican—Jan. 4, 2007

Rep. David P. Roe
of Johnson City (1st District)
Republican—5th term

Rep. John J. Duncan, Jr.
of Knoxville (2nd District)
Republican—16th term

TENNESSEE

Rep. Charles J. "Chuck" Fleischmann
of Chattanooga (3rd District)
Republican—4th term

Rep. Scott DesJarlais
of South Pittsburg (4th District)
Republican—4th term

Rep. Jim Cooper
of Nashville (5th District)
Democrat—14th term *

Rep. Diane Black
of Gallatin (6th District)
Republican—4th term

Rep. Marsha Blackburn
of Brentwood (7th District)
Republican—8th term

Rep. David Kustoff
of Germantown (8th District)
Republican—1st term

Rep. Steve Cohen
of Memphis (9th District)
Democrat—6th term

TEXAS

Sen. John Cornyn
of Austin
Republican—Jan. 7, 2003

Sen. Ted Cruz
of Houston
Republican—Jan. 3, 2013

Rep. Louie Gohmert
of Tyler (1st District)
Republican—7th term

Rep. Ted Poe
of Atascocita (2nd District)
Republican—7th term

Rep. Sam Johnson
of Plano (3rd District)
Republican—14th term

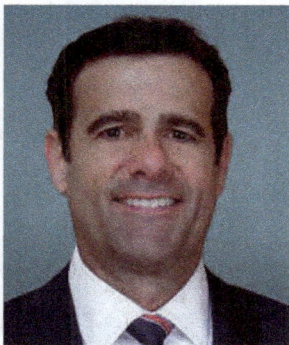

Rep. John Ratcliffe
of Heath (4th District)
Republican—2nd term

Rep. Jeb Hensarling
of Dallas (5th District)
Republican—8th term

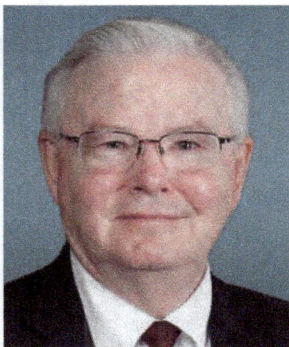

Rep. Joe Barton
of Ennis (6th District)
Republican—17th term

TEXAS

Rep. John Abney Culberson
of Houston (7th District)
Republican—9th term

Rep. Kevin Brady
of The Woodlands (8th District)
Republican—11th term

Rep. Al Green
of Houston (9th District)
Democrat—7th term

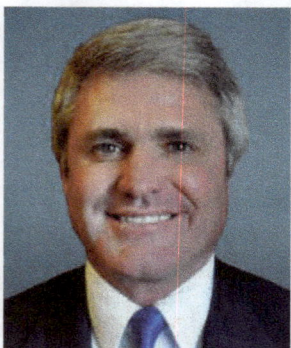

Rep. Michael T. McCaul
of Austin (10th District)
Republican—7th term

Rep. K. Michael Conaway
of Midland (11th District)
Republican—7th term

Rep. Kay Granger
of Fort Worth (12th District)
Republican—11th term

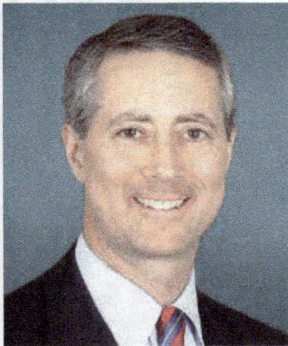

Rep. Mac Thornberry
of Clarendon (13th District)
Republican—12th term

Rep. Randy K. Weber, Sr.
of Friendswood (14th District)
Republican—3rd term

TEXAS

Rep. Vicente Gonzalez
of McAllen (15th District)
Democrat—1st term

Rep. Beto O'Rourke
of El Paso (16th District)
Democrat—3rd term

Rep. Bill Flores
of Bryan (17th District)
Republican—4th term

Rep. Sheila Jackson Lee
of Houston (18th District)
Democrat—12th term

Rep. Jodey C. Arrington
of Lubbock (19th District)
Republican—1st term

Rep. Joaquin Castro
of San Antonio (20th District)
Democrat—3rd term

Rep. Lamar Smith
of San Antonio (21st District)
Republican—16th term

Rep. Pete Olson
of Sugar Land (22nd District)
Republican—5th term

Rep. Will Hurd
of San Antonio (23rd District)
Republican—2nd term

Rep. Kenny Marchant
of Coppell (24th District)
Republican—7th term

Rep. Roger Williams
of Austin (25th District)
Republican—3rd term

Rep. Michael C. Burgess
of Pilot Point (26th District)
Republican—8th term

Rep. Blake Farenthold
of Corpus Christi (27th District)
Republican—4th term

Rep. Henry Cuellar
of Laredo (28th District)
Democrat—7th term

Rep. Gene Green
of Houston (29th District)
Democrat—13th term

Rep. Eddie Bernice Johnson
of Dallas (30th District)
Democrat—13th term

TEXAS

Rep. John R. Carter
of Round Rock (31st District)
Republican—8th term

Rep. Pete Sessions
of Dallas (32nd District)
Republican—11th term

Rep. Marc A. Veasey
of Fort Worth (33rd District)
Democrat—3rd term

Rep. Filemon Vela
of Brownsville (34th District)
Democrat—3rd term

Rep. Lloyd Doggett
of Austin (35th District)
Democrat—12th term

Rep. Brian Babin
of Woodville (36th District)
Republican—2nd term

UTAH

Sen. Orrin G. Hatch
of Salt Lake City
Republican—Jan. 3, 1977

Sen. Michael S. Lee
of Alpine
Republican—Jan. 5, 2011

Rep. Rob Bishop
of Brigham City (1st District)
Republican—8th term

Rep. Chris Stewart
of Farmington (2nd District)
Republican—3rd term

Rep. John R. Curtis
of Provo (3rd District)
Republican—1st term

Rep. Mia B. Love
of Saratoga Springs
  (4th District)
Republican—2nd term

VERMONT

Sen. Patrick J. Leahy
of Middlesex
Democrat—Jan. 3, 1975

Sen. Bernard Sanders
of Burlington
Independent—Jan. 4, 2007

Rep. Peter Welch
of Norwich (At Large)
Democrat—6th term

Sen. Mark R. Warner
of Alexandria
Democrat—Jan. 6, 2009

Sen. Tim Kaine
of Richmond
Democrat—Jan. 3, 2013

Rep. Robert J. Wittman
of Montross (1st District)
Republican—6th term

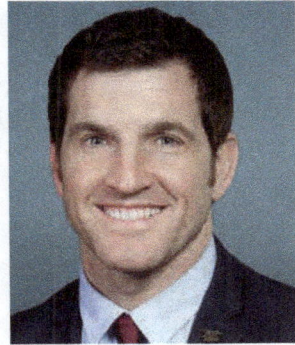

Rep. Scott Taylor
of Virginia Beach (2nd District)
Republican—1st term

VIRGINIA

Rep. Robert C. "Bobby" Scott
of Newport News (3rd District)
Democrat—13th term

Rep. A. Donald McEachin
of Henrico (4th District)
Democrat—1st term

Rep. Thomas A. Garrett, Jr.
of Scottsville (5th District)
Republican—1st term

Rep. Bob Goodlatte
of Roanoke (6th District)
Republican—13th term

Rep. Dave Brat
of Glen Allen (7th District)
Republican—3rd term

Rep. Donald S. Beyer, Jr.
of Alexandria (8th District)
Democrat—2nd term

Rep. H. Morgan Griffith
of Salem (9th District)
Republican—4th term

Rep. Barbara Comstock
of McLean (10th District)
Republican—2nd term

VIRGINIA

Rep. Gerald E. Connolly
of Fairfax (11th District)
Democrat—5th term

Sen. Patty Murray
of Seattle
Democrat—Jan. 3, 1993

Sen. Maria Cantwell
of Edmonds
Democrat—Jan. 3, 2001

Rep. Suzan K. DelBene
of Medina (1st District)
Democrat—4th term

Rep. Rick Larsen
of Everett (2nd District)
Democrat—9th term

WASHINGTON

Rep. Jaime Herrera Beutler
of Battle Ground (3rd District)
Republican—4th term

Rep. Dan Newhouse
of Sunnyside (4th District)
Republican—2nd term

Rep. Cathy McMorris Rodgers
of Spokane (5th District)
Republican—7th term

Rep. Derek Kilmer
of Gig Harbor (6th District)
Democrat—3rd term

Rep. Pramila Jayapal
of Seattle (7th District)
Democrat—1st term

Rep. David G. Reichert
of Auburn (8th District)
Republican—7th term

Rep. Adam Smith
of Bellevue (9th District)
Democrat—11th term

Rep. Denny Heck
of Olympia (10th District)
Democrat—3rd term

WEST VIRGINIA

Sen. Joe Manchin III
of Fairmont
Democrat—Nov. 15, 2010

Sen. Shelley Moore Capito
of Charleston
Republican—Jan. 6, 2015

Rep. David B. McKinley
of Wheeling (1st District)
Republican—4th term

Rep. Alexander X. Mooney
of Charles Town (2nd District)
Republican—2nd term

Rep. Evan H. Jenkins
of Huntington (3rd District)
Republican—2nd term

WISCONSIN

Sen. Ron Johnson
of Oshkosh
Republican—Jan. 5, 2011

Sen. Tammy Baldwin
of Madison
Democrat—Jan. 3, 2013

Rep. Paul D. Ryan
of Janesville (1st District)
Republican—10th term

Rep. Mark Pocan
of Madison (2nd District)
Democrat—3rd term

Rep. Ron Kind
of La Crosse (3rd District)
Democrat—11th term

Rep. Gwen Moore
of Milwaukee (4th District)
Democrat—7th term

**Rep. F. James
   Sensenbrenner, Jr.**
*of Menomonee Falls
   (5th District)*
Republican—20th term

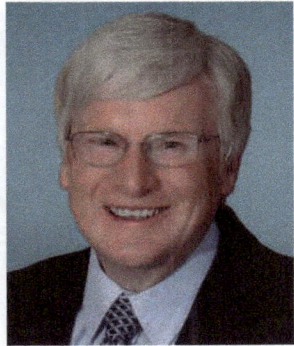

Rep. Glenn Grothman
of Glenbeulah (6th District)
Republican—2nd term

WISCONSIN

Rep. Sean P. Duffy
of Wausau (7th District)
Republican—4th term

Rep. Mike Gallagher
of Green Bay (8th District)
Republican—1st term

Sen. Michael B. Enzi
of Gillette
Republican—Jan. 7, 1997

Sen. John A. Barrasso
of Casper
Republican—Jun. 25, 2007

Rep. Liz Cheney
of Wilson (At Large)
Republican—1st term

Aumua Amata Coleman Radewagen
of Pago Pago, American Samoa
Republican—2nd term

Eleanor Holmes Norton
of District of Columbia
Democrat—14th term

Madeleine Z. Bordallo
of Hagatna, Guam
Democrat—8th term

Gregorio Kilili Camacho Sablan
of Saipan, Northern Mariana Islands
Democrat—5th term

Jenniffer González-Colón
of San Juan, Puerto Rico
Republican—1st term ††

Stacey E. Plaskett
of St. Croix, Virgin Islands
Democrat—2nd term

STATE
DELEGATIONS

State Delegations

Number which precedes name of Representative designates Congressional district.
Republicans in roman; Democrats in *italic*; Independent in **bold**

ALABAMA

SENATORS

Richard C. Shelby   *Doug Jones*

REPRESENTATIVES
[Republican, 6; Democrat, 1]

1. Bradley Byrne
2. Martha Roby
3. Mike Rogers
4. Robert B. Aderholt
5. Mo Brooks
6. Gary J. Palmer
7. *Terri A. Sewell*

ALASKA

SENATORS

Lisa Murkowski   Dan Sullivan

REPRESENTATIVES
[Republican, 1]

At Large—Don Young

STATE DELEGATIONS

ARIZONA

SENATORS

John McCain   Jeff Flake

REPRESENTATIVES
[Republican, 4; Democrat, 4]

1. *Tom O'Halleran*
2. Martha McSally
3. *Raúl M. Grijalva*
4. Paul A. Gosar
5. Andy Biggs

6. David Schweikert
7. *Ruben Gallego*
8. Vacant
9. *Kyrsten Sinema*

ARKANSAS

SENATORS

John Boozman   Tom Cotton

REPRESENTATIVES
[Republican, 4]

1. Eric A. "Rick" Crawford
2. J. French Hill

3. Steve Womack
4. Bruce Westerman

CALIFORNIA

SENATORS

Dianne Feinstein   *Kamala D. Harris*

REPRESENTATIVES

[Republican, 14; Democrat, 39]

1. Doug LaMalfa
2. *Jared Huffman*
3. *John Garamendi*
4. Tom McClintock
5. *Mike Thompson*
6. *Doris O. Matsui*
7. *Ami Bera*
8. Paul Cook
9. *Jerry McNerney*
10. Jeff Denham
11. *Mark DeSaulnier*
12. *Nancy Pelosi*
13. *Barbara Lee*
14. *Jackie Speier*
15. *Eric Swalwell*
16. *Jim Costa*
17. *Ro Khanna*
18. *Anna G. Eshoo*
19. *Zoe Lofgren*
20. *Jimmy Panetta*
21. David G. Valadao
22. Devin Nunes
23. Kevin McCarthy
24. *Salud O. Carbajal*
25. Stephen Knight
26. *Julia Brownley*
27. *Judy Chu*
28. *Adam B. Schiff*
29. *Tony Cárdenas*
30. *Brad Sherman*
31. *Pete Aguilar*
32. *Grace F. Napolitano*
33. *Ted Lieu*
34. *Jimmy Gomez*
35. *Norma J. Torres*
36. *Raul Ruiz*
37. *Karen Bass*
38. *Linda T. Sánchez*
39. Edward R. Royce
40. *Lucille Roybal-Allard*
41. *Mark Takano*
42. Ken Calvert
43. *Maxine Waters*
44. *Nanette Diaz Barragán*
45. Mimi Walters
46. *J. Luis Correa*
47. *Alan S. Lowenthal*
48. Dana Rohrabacher
49. Darrell E. Issa
50. Duncan Hunter
51. *Juan Vargas*
52. *Scott H. Peters*
53. *Susan A. Davis*

COLORADO

SENATORS

Michael F. Bennet   Cory Gardner

REPRESENTATIVES
[Republican, 4; Democrat, 3]

1. *Diana DeGette*
2. *Jared Polis*
3. Scott R. Tipton
4. Ken Buck

5. Doug Lamborn
6. Mike Coffman
7. *Ed Perlmutter*

CONNECTICUT

SENATORS

Richard Blumenthal   *Christopher S. Murphy*

REPRESENTATIVES
[Democrat, 5]

1. *John B. Larson*
2. *Joe Courtney*
3. *Rosa L. DeLauro*

4. *James A. Himes*
5. *Elizabeth H. Esty*

DELAWARE

SENATORS

Thomas R. Carper   Christopher A. Coons

REPRESENTATIVES
[Democrat, 1]

At Large—*Lisa Blunt Rochester*

FLORIDA

SENATORS

Bill Nelson   Marco Rubio

REPRESENTATIVES
[Republican, 16; Democrat, 11]

1. Matt Gaetz
2. Neal P. Dunn
3. Ted S. Yoho
4. John H. Rutherford
5. *Al Lawson, Jr.*
6. Ron DeSantis
7. *Stephanie N. Murphy*
8. Bill Posey
9. *Darren Soto*
10. *Val Butler Demings*
11. Daniel Webster
12. Gus M. Bilirakis
13. *Charlie Crist*
14. *Kathy Castor*
15. Dennis A. Ross
16. Vern Buchanan
17. Thomas J. Rooney
18. Brian J. Mast
19. Francis Rooney
20. *Alcee L. Hastings*
21. *Lois Frankel*
22. *Theodore E. Deutch*
23. *Debbie Wasserman Schultz*
24. *Frederica S. Wilson*
25. Mario Diaz-Balart
26. Carlos Curbelo
27. Ileana Ros-Lehtinen

GEORGIA

SENATORS

Johnny Isakson   David Perdue

REPRESENTATIVES
[Republican, 10; Democrat, 4]

1. Earl L. "Buddy" Carter
2. *Sanford D. Bishop, Jr.*
3. A. Drew Ferguson IV
4. *Henry C. "Hank" Johnson, Jr.*
5. *John Lewis*
6. Karen C. Handel
7. Rob Woodall
8. Austin Scott
9. Doug Collins
10. Jody B. Hice
11. Barry Loudermilk
12. Rick W. Allen
13. *David Scott*
14. Tom Graves

STATE DELEGATIONS

HAWAII

SENATORS

Brian E. Schatz   Mazie K. Hirono

REPRESENTATIVES
[Democrat, 2]

1. Colleen Hanabusa   2. Tulsi Gabbard

IDAHO

SENATORS

Mike Crapo   James E. Risch

REPRESENTATIVES
[Republican, 2]

1. Raúl R. Labrador   2. Michael K. Simpson

ILLINOIS

SENATORS

Richard J. Durbin   Tammy Duckworth

REPRESENTATIVES
[Republican, 7; Democrat, 11]

1. Bobby L. Rush   10. Bradley Scott Schneider
2. Robin L. Kelly   11. Bill Foster
3. Daniel Lipinski   12. Mike Bost
4. Luis V. Gutiérrez   13. Rodney Davis
5. Mike Quigley   14. Randy Hultgren
6. Peter J. Roskam   15. John Shimkus
7. Danny K. Davis   16. Adam Kinzinger
8. Raja Krishnamoorthi   17. Cheri Bustos
9. Janice D. Schakowsky   18. Darin LaHood

INDIANA

SENATORS

Joe Donnelly   Todd Young

REPRESENTATIVES
[Republican, 7; Democrat, 2]

1. *Peter J. Visclosky*
2. Jackie Walorski
3. Jim Banks
4. Todd Rokita
5. Susan W. Brooks
6. Luke Messer
7. *André Carson*
8. Larry Bucshon
9. Trey Hollingsworth

IOWA

SENATORS

Chuck Grassley   Joni Ernst

REPRESENTATIVES
[Republican, 3; Democrat, 1]

1. Rod Blum
2. *David Loebsack*
3. David Young
4. Steve King

KANSAS

SENATORS

Pat Roberts   Jerry Moran

REPRESENTATIVES
[Republican, 4]

1. Roger W. Marshall
2. Lynn Jenkins
3. Kevin Yoder
4. Ron Estes

KENTUCKY

SENATORS

Mitch McConnell   Rand Paul

REPRESENTATIVES
[Republican, 5; Democrat, 1]

1. James Comer
2. Brett Guthrie
3. *John A. Yarmuth*

4. Thomas Massie
5. Harold Rogers
6. Andy Barr

LOUISIANA

SENATORS

Bill Cassidy, M.D.   John Kennedy

REPRESENTATIVES
[Republican, 5; Democrat, 1]

1. Steve Scalise
2. *Cedric L. Richmond*
3. Clay Higgins

4. Mike Johnson
5. Ralph Lee Abraham
6. Garret Graves

MAINE

SENATORS

Susan M. Collins   **Angus S. King, Jr.**

REPRESENTATIVES
[Republican, 1; Democrat, 1]

1. *Chellie Pingree*   2. Bruce Poliquin

MARYLAND

SENATORS

Benjamin L. Cardin   *Chris Van Hollen*

REPRESENTATIVES
[Republican, 1; Democrat, 7]

1. Andy Harris
2. *C.A. Dutch Ruppersberger*
3. *John P. Sarbanes*
4. *Anthony G. Brown*
5. *Steny H. Hoyer*
6. *John K. Delaney*
7. *Elijah E. Cummings*
8. *Jamie Raskin*

MASSACHUSETTS

SENATORS

Elizabeth Warren   *Edward J. Markey*

REPRESENTATIVES
[Democrat, 9]

1. *Richard E. Neal*
2. *James P. McGovern*
3. *Niki Tsongas*
4. *Joseph P. Kennedy III*
5. *Katherine M. Clark*
6. *Seth Moulton*
7. *Michael E. Capuano*
8. *Stephen F. Lynch*
9. *William R. Keating*

MICHIGAN

SENATORS

Debbie Stabenow   Gary C. Peters

REPRESENTATIVES
[Republican, 9; Democrat, 4]

1. Jack Bergman
2. Bill Huizenga
3. Justin Amash
4. John R. Moolenaar
5. *Daniel T. Kildee*
6. Fred Upton
7. Tim Walberg
8. Mike Bishop
9. *Sander M. Levin*
10. Paul Mitchell
11. David A. Trott
12. *Debbie Dingell*
13. Vacant
14. *Brenda L. Lawrence*

MINNESOTA

SENATORS

Amy Klobuchar   *Tina Smith*

REPRESENTATIVES
[Republican, 3; Democrat, 5]

1. *Timothy J. Walz*
2. Jason Lewis
3. Erik Paulsen
4. *Betty McCollum*
5. *Keith Ellison*
6. Tom Emmer
7. *Collin C. Peterson*
8. *Richard M. Nolan*

MISSISSIPPI

SENATORS

Thad Cochran   Roger F. Wicker

REPRESENTATIVES
[Republican, 3; Democrat, 1]

1. Trent Kelly
2. *Bennie G. Thompson*
3. Gregg Harper
4. Steven M. Palazzo

MISSOURI

SENATORS

Claire McCaskill   Roy Blunt

REPRESENTATIVES
[Republican, 6; Democrat, 2]

1. *Wm. Lacy Clay*
2. Ann Wagner
3. Blaine Luetkemeyer
4. Vicky Hartzler
5. *Emanuel Cleaver*
6. Sam Graves
7. Billy Long
8. Jason Smith

MONTANA

SENATORS

Jon Tester   Steve Daines

REPRESENTATIVES
[Republican, 1]

At Large—Greg Gianforte

NEBRASKA

SENATORS

Deb Fischer   Ben Sasse

REPRESENTATIVES
[Republican, 3]

1. Jeff Fortenberry
2. Don Bacon
3. Adrian Smith

NEVADA

SENATORS

Dean Heller   *Catherine Cortez Masto*

REPRESENTATIVES
[Republican, 1; Democrat, 3]

1. *Dina Titus*
2. Mark E. Amodei
3. *Jacky Rosen*
4. *Ruben J. Kihuen*

NEW HAMPSHIRE

SENATORS

Jeanne Shaheen   *Maggie Hassan*

REPRESENTATIVES
[Democrat, 2]

1. *Carol Shea-Porter*
2. *Ann M. Kuster*

NEW JERSEY

SENATORS

Robert Menendez   *Cory A. Booker*

REPRESENTATIVES
[Republican, 5; Democrat, 7]

1. *Donald Norcross*
2. Frank A. LoBiondo
3. Thomas MacArthur
4. Christopher H. Smith
5. *Josh Gottheimer*
6. *Frank Pallone, Jr.*
7. Leonard Lance
8. *Albio Sires*
9. *Bill Pascrell, Jr.*
10. *Donald M. Payne, Jr.*
11. Rodney P. Frelinghuysen
12. *Bonnie Watson Coleman*

NEW MEXICO

SENATORS

Tom Udall   *Martin Heinrich*

REPRESENTATIVES
[Republican, 1; Democrat, 2]

1. *Michelle Lujan Grisham*   3. *Ben Ray Luján*
2. Stevan Pearce

NEW YORK

SENATORS

Charles E. Schumer   *Kirsten Gillibrand*

REPRESENTATIVES
[Republican, 9; Democrat, 18]

1. Lee M. Zeldin   15. *José E. Serrano*
2. Peter T. King   16. *Eliot L. Engel*
3. *Thomas R. Suozzi*   17. *Nita M. Lowey*
4. *Kathleen M. Rice*   18. *Sean Patrick Maloney*
5. *Gregory W. Meeks*   19. John J. Faso
6. *Grace Meng*   20. *Paul Tonko*
7. *Nydia M. Velázquez*   21. Elise M. Stefanik
8. *Hakeem S. Jeffries*   22. Claudia Tenney
9. *Yvette D. Clarke*   23. Tom Reed
10. *Jerrold Nadler*   24. John Katko
11. Daniel M. Donovan, Jr.   25. *Louise McIntosh Slaughter*
12. *Carolyn B. Maloney*   26. *Brian Higgins*
13. *Adriano Espaillat*   27. Chris Collins
14. *Joseph Crowley*

NORTH CAROLINA

SENATORS

Richard Burr   Thom Tillis

REPRESENTATIVES
[Republican, 10; Democrat, 3]

1. *G.K. Butterfield*
2. George Holding
3. Walter B. Jones
4. *David E. Price*
5. Virginia Foxx
6. Mark Walker
7. David Rouzer
8. Richard Hudson
9. Robert Pittenger
10. Patrick T. McHenry
11. Mark Meadows
12. *Alma S. Adams*
13. Ted Budd

NORTH DAKOTA

SENATORS

John Hoeven   *Heidi Heitkamp*

REPRESENTATIVES
[Republican, 1]

At Large—Kevin Cramer

OHIO

SENATORS

Sherrod Brown   Rob Portman

REPRESENTATIVES
[Republican, 11; Democrat, 4]

1. Steve Chabot
2. Brad R. Wenstrup
3. *Joyce Beatty*
4. Jim Jordan
5. Robert E. Latta
6. Bill Johnson
7. Bob Gibbs
8. Warren Davidson
9. *Marcy Kaptur*
10. Michael R. Turner
11. *Marcia L. Fudge*
12. Vacant
13. *Tim Ryan*
14. David P. Joyce
15. Steve Stivers
16. James B. Renacci

OKLAHOMA

SENATORS

James M. Inhofe   James Lankford

REPRESENTATIVES
[Republican, 5]

1. Jim Bridenstine
2. Markwayne Mullin
3. Frank D. Lucas
4. Tom Cole
5. Steve Russell

OREGON

SENATORS

Ron Wyden   *Jeff Merkley*

REPRESENTATIVES
[Republican, 1; Democrat, 4]

1. *Suzanne Bonamici*
2. Greg Walden
3. *Earl Blumenauer*
4. *Peter A. DeFazio*
5. *Kurt Schrader*

PENNSYLVANIA

SENATORS

Robert P. Casey, Jr.   Pat Toomey

REPRESENTATIVES
[Republican, 12; Democrat, 5]

1. *Robert A. Brady*
2. *Dwight Evans*
3. Mike Kelly
4. Scott Perry
5. Glenn Thompson
6. Ryan A. Costello
7. Patrick Meehan
8. Brian K. Fitzpatrick
9. Bill Shuster
10. Tom Marino
11. Lou Barletta
12. Keith J. Rothfus
13. *Brendan F. Boyle*
14. *Michael F. Doyle*
15. Charles W. Dent
16. Lloyd Smucker
17. *Matt Cartwright*
18. Vacant

RHODE ISLAND

SENATORS

Jack Reed   *Sheldon Whitehouse*

REPRESENTATIVES
[Democrat, 2]

1. *David N. Cicilline*
2. *James R. Langevin*

SOUTH CAROLINA

SENATORS

Lindsey Graham   Tim Scott

REPRESENTATIVES
[Republican, 6; Democrat, 1]

1. Mark Sanford
2. Joe Wilson
3. Jeff Duncan
4. Trey Gowdy

5. Ralph Norman
6. *James E. Clyburn*
7. Tom Rice

SOUTH DAKOTA

SENATORS

John Thune   Mike Rounds

REPRESENTATIVES
[Republican, 1]

At Large—Kristi L. Noem

TENNESSEE

SENATORS

Lamar Alexander   Bob Corker

REPRESENTATIVES
[Republican, 7; Democrat, 2]

1. David P. Roe
2. John J. Duncan, Jr.
3. Charles J. "Chuck"
   Fleischmann
4. Scott DesJarlais

5. *Jim Cooper*
6. Diane Black
7. Marsha Blackburn
8. David Kustoff
9. *Steve Cohen*

TEXAS

SENATORS

John Cornyn   Ted Cruz

REPRESENTATIVES
[Republican, 25; Democrat, 11]

1. Louie Gohmert
2. Ted Poe
3. Sam Johnson
4. John Ratcliffe
5. Jeb Hensarling
6. Joe Barton
7. John Abney Culberson
8. Kevin Brady
9. *Al Green*
10. Michael T. McCaul
11. K. Michael Conaway
12. Kay Granger
13. Mac Thornberry
14. Randy K. Weber, Sr.
15. *Vicente Gonzalez*
16. *Beto O'Rourke*
17. Bill Flores
18. *Sheila Jackson Lee*
19. Jodey C. Arrington
20. *Joaquin Castro*
21. Lamar Smith
22. Pete Olson
23. Will Hurd
24. Kenny Marchant
25. Roger Williams
26. Michael C. Burgess
27. Blake Farenthold
28. *Henry Cuellar*
29. *Gene Green*
30. *Eddie Bernice Johnson*
31. John R. Carter
32. Pete Sessions
33. *Marc A. Veasey*
34. *Filemon Vela*
35. *Lloyd Doggett*
36. Brian Babin

UTAH

SENATORS

Orrin G. Hatch   Michael S. Lee

REPRESENTATIVES
[Republican, 4]

1. Rob Bishop
2. Chris Stewart
3. John R. Curtis
4. Mia B. Love

VERMONT

SENATORS

Patrick J. Leahy   **Bernard Sanders**

REPRESENTATIVES

[Democrat, 1]

At Large—*Peter Welch*

VIRGINIA

SENATORS

Mark R. Warner   *Tim Kaine*

REPRESENTATIVES

[Republican, 7; Democrat, 4]

1. Robert J. Wittman
2. Scott Taylor
3. *Robert C. "Bobby" Scott*
4. *A. Donald McEachin*
5. Thomas A. Garrett, Jr.
6. Bob Goodlatte
7. Dave Brat
8. *Donald S. Beyer, Jr.*
9. H. Morgan Griffith
10. Barbara Comstock
11. *Gerald E. Connolly*

WASHINGTON

SENATORS

Patty Murray   *Maria Cantwell*

REPRESENTATIVES

[Republican, 4; Democrat, 6]

1. *Suzan K. DelBene*
2. *Rick Larsen*
3. Jaime Herrera Beutler
4. Dan Newhouse
5. Cathy McMorris Rodgers
6. *Derek Kilmer*
7. *Pramila Jayapal*
8. David G. Reichert
9. *Adam Smith*
10. *Denny Heck*

STATE DELEGATIONS

WEST VIRGINIA

SENATORS

Joe Manchin III   Shelley Moore Capito

REPRESENTATIVES
[Republican, 3]

1. David B. McKinley   3. Evan H. Jenkins
2. Alexander X. Mooney

WISCONSIN

SENATORS

Ron Johnson   *Tammy Baldwin*

REPRESENTATIVES
[Republican, 5; Democrat, 3]

1. Paul D. Ryan   5. F. James Sensenbrenner, Jr.
2. *Mark Pocan*   6. Glenn Grothman
3. *Ron Kind*   7. Sean P. Duffy
4. *Gwen Moore*   8. Mike Gallagher

WYOMING

SENATORS

Michael B. Enzi   John A. Barrasso

REPRESENTATIVES
[Republican, 1]

At Large—Liz Cheney

AMERICAN SAMOA

DELEGATE

[Republican, 1]

Aumua Amata Coleman Radewagen

DISTRICT OF COLUMBIA

DELEGATE

[Democrat, 1]

Eleanor Holmes Norton

GUAM

DELEGATE

[Democrat, 1]

Madeleine Z. Bordallo

NORTHERN MARIANA ISLANDS

DELEGATE

[Democrat, 1]

Gregorio Kilili Camacho Sablan

PUERTO RICO

RESIDENT COMMISSIONER

[Republican, 1]

Jenniffer González-Colón

VIRGIN ISLANDS OF THE UNITED STATES

DELEGATE

[Democrat, 1]

Stacey E. Plaskett

PARTY DIVISION

SENATE

Republicans	51
Democrats	47
Independent	2
Total	100

HOUSE

Republicans	238
Democrats	193
Vacant	4
Total	435

ALPHABETICAL
LISTS

Alphabetical Lists

Alphabetical list of Senators, Representatives, Delegates, and Resident Commissioner, showing home post office and political alignment.

SENATORS

Republicans in roman(51); Democrats in *italic* (47);

Independent in **bold** (2); total, 100

Name	Home post office
Alexander, Lamar	Maryville, TN
Baldwin, Tammy	Madison, WI
Barrasso, John A.	Casper, WY
Bennet, Michael F.	Denver, CO
Blumenthal, Richard	Greenwich, CT
Blunt, Roy	Springfield, MO
Booker, Cory A.	Newark, NJ
Boozman, John	Rogers, AR
Brown, Sherrod	Cleveland, OH
Burr, Richard	Winston-Salem, NC
Cantwell, Maria	Edmonds, WA
Capito, Shelley Moore	Charleston, WV
Cardin, Benjamin L.	Baltimore, MD
Carper, Thomas R.	Wilmington, DE
Casey, Robert P., Jr.	Scranton, PA
Cassidy, Bill, M.D.	Baton Rouge, LA
Cochran, Thad.	Oxford, MS
Collins, Susan M..	Bangor, ME
Coons, Christopher A..	Wilmington, DE
Corker, Bob	Chattanooga, TN
Cornyn, John.	Austin, TX
Cortez Masto, Catherine	Las Vegas, NV

SENATORS

Name	Home post office
Cotton, Tom	Dardanelle, AR
Crapo, Mike	Idaho Falls, ID
Cruz, Ted	Houston, TX
Daines, Steve	Bozeman, MT
Donnelly, Joe	Granger, IN
Duckworth, Tammy	Hoffman Estates, IL
Durbin, Richard J.	Springfield, IL
Enzi, Michael B.	Gillette, WY
Ernst, Joni	Red Oak, IA
Feinstein, Dianne	San Francisco, CA
Fischer, Deb	Valentine, NE
Flake, Jeff	Mesa, AZ
Gardner, Cory	Yuma, CO
Gillibrand, Kirsten	Brunswick, NY
Graham, Lindsey	Seneca, SC
Grassley, Chuck	New Hartford, IA
Harris, Kamala D.	Oakland, CA
Hassan, Maggie	Newfields, NH
Hatch, Orrin G.	Salt Lake City, UT
Heinrich, Martin	Albuquerque, NM
Heitkamp, Heidi	Mantador, ND
Heller, Dean	Carson City, NV
Hirono, Mazie K.	Honolulu, HI
Hoeven, John	Bismarck, ND
Inhofe, James M.	Tulsa, OK
Isakson, Johnny	Marietta, GA
Johnson, Ron	Oshkosh, WI
Jones, Doug	Fairfield, AL
Kaine, Tim	Richmond, VA
Kennedy, John	Madisonville, LA
King, Angus S., Jr.	Brunswick, ME
Klobuchar, Amy	Minneapolis, MN
Lankford, James	Edmond, OK
Leahy, Patrick J.	Middlesex, VT
Lee, Michael S.	Alpine, UT

Name	Home post office
Manchin, Joe III	Fairmont, WV
Markey, Edward J.	Malden, MA
McCain, John	Phoenix, AZ
McCaskill, Claire	Kirkwood, MO
McConnell, Mitch	Louisville, KY
Menendez, Robert	North Bergen, NJ
Merkley, Jeff	East Portland, OR
Moran, Jerry	Manhattan, KS
Murkowski, Lisa	Girdwood, AK
Murphy, Christopher S.	Cheshire, CT
Murray, Patty	Seattle, WA
Nelson, Bill	Orlando, FL
Paul, Rand	Bowling Green, KY
Perdue, David	Glynn County, GA
Peters, Gary C.	Bloomfield Hills, MI
Portman, Rob	Terrace Park, OH
Reed, Jack	Jamestown, RI
Risch, James E.	Boise, ID
Roberts, Pat	Dodge City, KS
Rounds, Mike	Huron, SD
Rubio, Marco	Miami, FL
Sanders, Bernard	Burlington, VT
Sasse, Ben	Fremont, NE
Schatz, Brian E.	Honolulu, HI
Schumer, Charles E.	Brooklyn, NY
Scott, Tim	North Charleston, SC
Shaheen, Jeanne	Madbury, NH
Shelby, Richard C.	Tuscaloosa, AL
Smith, Tina	Minneapolis, MN
Stabenow, Debbie	Lansing, MI
Sullivan, Dan.	Anchorage, AK
Tester, Jon	Big Sandy, MT
Thune, John	Murdo, SD
Tillis, Thom	Huntersville, NC
Toomey, Pat	Zionsville, PA

SENATORS

REPRESENTATIVES

Republicans in roman (238); Democrats in *italic* (193); vacant (4); total, 435

Name	Home post office/Dist. no.
Abraham, Ralph Lee	Alto, LA (5th)
Adams, Alma S.	Charlotte, NC (12th)
Aderholt, Robert B.	Haleyville, AL (4th)
Aguilar, Pete	Redlands, CA (31st)
Allen, Rick W.	Augusta, GA (12th)
Amash, Justin	Cascade Township, MI (3rd)
Amodei, Mark E.	Carson City, NV (2nd)
Arrington, Jodey C.	Lubbock, TX (19th)
Babin, Brian	Woodville, TX (36th)
Bacon, Don	Papillion, NE (2nd)
Banks, Jim	Columbia City, IN (3rd)
Barletta, Lou	Hazleton, PA (11th)
Barr, Andy	Lexington, KY (6th)
Barragán, Nanette Diaz	San Pedro, CA (44th)
Barton, Joe	Ennis, TX (6th)
Bass, Karen	Los Angeles, CA (37th)
Beatty, Joyce	Columbus, OH (3rd)
Bera, Ami	Elk Grove, CA (7th)
Bergman, Jack	Watersmeet, MI (1st)
Beyer, Donald S., Jr.	Alexandria, VA (8th)
Biggs, Andy	Gilbert, AZ (5th)
Bilirakis, Gus M.	Palm Harbor, FL (12th)
Bishop, Mike	Rochester, MI (8th)
Bishop, Rob	Brigham City, UT (1st)
Bishop, Sanford D., Jr.	Albany, GA (2nd)
Black, Diane	Gallatin, TN (6th)
Blackburn, Marsha	Brentwood, TN (7th)
Blum, Rod	Dubuque, IA (1st)
Blumenauer, Earl	Portland, OR (3rd)
Blunt Rochester, Lisa	Wilmington, DE (At Large)

REPRESENTATIVES

Name	Home post office/Dist. no.
Bonamici, Suzanne	Washington County, OR (1st)
Bost, Mike	Murphysboro, IL (12th)
Boyle, Brendan F.	Philadelphia, PA (13th)
Brady, Kevin	The Woodlands, TX (8th)
Brady, Robert A.	Philadelphia, PA (1st)
Brat, Dave	Glen Allen, VA (7th)
Bridenstine, Jim	Tulsa, OK (1st)
Brooks, Mo.	Huntsville, AL (5th)
Brooks, Susan W.	Carmel, IN (5th)
Brown, Anthony G.	Mitchellville, MD (4th)
Brownley, Julia	Westlake Village, CA (26th)
Buchanan, Vern	Sarasota, FL (16th)
Buck, Ken	Windsor, CO (4th)
Bucshon, Larry	Newburgh, IN (8th)
Budd, Ted	Advance, NC (13th)
Burgess, Michael C.	Pilot Point, TX (26th)
Bustos, Cheri	Moline, IL (17th)
Butterfield, G.K.	Wilson, NC (1st)
Byrne, Bradley	Fairhope, AL (1st)
Calvert, Ken	Corona, CA (42nd)
Capuano, Michael E.	Somerville, MA (7th)
Carbajal, Salud O.	Santa Barbara, CA (24th)
Cárdenas, Tony	Pacoima, CA (29th)
Carson, André	Indianapolis, IN (7th)
Carter, Earl L. "Buddy"	Pooler, GA (1st)
Carter, John R.	Round Rock, TX (31st)
Cartwright, Matt	Moosic, PA (17th)
Castor, Kathy	Tampa, FL (14th)
Castro, Joaquin	San Antonio, TX (20th)
Chabot, Steve	Cincinnati, OH (1st)
Cheney, Liz.	Wilson, WY (At Large)
Chu, Judy.	Monterey Park, CA (27th)
Cicilline, David N.	Providence, RI (1st)
Clark, Katherine M.	Melrose, MA (5th)
Clarke, Yvette D.	Brooklyn, NY (9th)

Name	Home post office/Dist. no.
Clay, Wm. Lacy	St. Louis, MO (1st)
Cleaver, Emanuel	Kansas City, MO (5th)
Clyburn, James E.	Columbia, SC (6th)
Coffman, Mike	Aurora, CO (6th)
Cohen, Steve	Memphis, TN (9th)
Cole, Tom	Moore, OK (4th)
Collins, Chris	Clarence, NY (27th)
Collins, Doug	Gainesville, GA (9th)
Comer, James	Tompkinsville, KY (1st)
Comstock, Barbara	McLean, VA (10th)
Conaway, K. Michael	Midland, TX (11th)
Connolly, Gerald E.	Fairfax, VA (11th)
Cook, Paul	Yucca Valley, CA (8th)
Cooper, Jim	Nashville, TN (5th)
Correa, J. Luis	Santa Ana, CA (46th)
Costa, Jim	Fresno, CA (16th)
Costello, Ryan A.	West Chester, PA (6th)
Courtney, Joe	Vernon, CT (2nd)
Cramer, Kevin	Bismarck, ND (At Large)
Crawford, Eric A. "Rick"	Jonesboro, AR (1st)
Crist, Charlie	St. Petersburg, FL (13th)
Crowley, Joseph	Queens/Bronx, NY (14th)
Cuellar, Henry	Laredo, TX (28th)
Culberson, John Abney	Houston, TX (7th)
Cummings, Elijah E.	Baltimore, MD (7th)
Curbelo, Carlos	Miami, FL (26th)
Curtis, John R.	Provo, UT (3rd)
Davidson, Warren	Troy, OH (8th)
Davis, Danny K.	Chicago, IL (7th)
Davis, Rodney	Taylorville, IL (13th)
Davis, Susan A.	San Diego, CA (53rd)
DeFazio, Peter A.	Springfield, OR (4th)
DeGette, Diana	Denver, CO (1st)
Delaney, John K.	Potomac, MD (6th)
DeLauro, Rosa L.	New Haven, CT (3rd)

REPRESENTATIVES

Name	Home post office/Dist. no.
DelBene, Suzan K.	Medina, WA (1st)
Demings, Val Butler	Orlando, FL (10th)
Denham, Jeff	Turlock, CA (10th)
Dent, Charles W..	Allentown, PA (15th)
DeSantis, Ron	Palm Coast, FL (6th)
DeSaulnier, Mark	Concord, CA (11th)
DesJarlais, Scott	South Pittsburg, TN (4th)
Deutch, Theodore E..	Boca Raton, FL (22nd)
Diaz-Balart, Mario.	Miami, FL (25th)
Dingell, Debbie	Dearborn, MI (12th)
Doggett, Lloyd	Austin, TX (35th)
Donovan, Daniel M., Jr.	Staten Island, NY (11th)
Doyle, Michael F.	Pittsburgh, PA (14th)
Duffy, Sean P.	Wausau, WI (7th)
Duncan, Jeff	Laurens, SC (3rd)
Duncan, John J., Jr.	Knoxville, TN (2nd)
Dunn, Neal P.	Panama City, FL (2nd)
Ellison, Keith	Minneapolis, MN (5th)
Emmer, Tom.	Delano, MN (6th)
Engel, Eliot L.	Bronx, NY (16th)
Eshoo, Anna G.	Atherton, CA (18th)
Espaillat, Adriano.	New York, NY (13th)
Estes, Ron	Wichita, KS (4th)
Esty, Elizabeth H.	Cheshire, CT (5th)
Evans, Dwight	Philadelphia, PA (2nd)
Farenthold, Blake	Corpus Christi, TX (27th)
Faso, John J.	Kinderhook, NY (19th)
Ferguson, A. Drew IV	West Point, GA (3rd)
Fitzpatrick, Brian K..	Levittown, PA (8th)
Fleischmann, Charles J. "Chuck"	Chattanooga, TN (3rd)
Flores, Bill	Bryan, TX (17th)
Fortenberry, Jeff.	Lincoln, NE (1st)
Foster, Bill	Naperville, IL (11th)
Foxx, Virginia	Banner Elk, NC (5th)
Frankel, Lois	West Palm Beach, FL (21st)

Name	Home post office/Dist. no.
Frelinghuysen, Rodney P.	Morristown, NJ (11th)
Fudge, Marcia L.	Warrensville Heights, OH (11th)
Gabbard, Tulsi	Kailua, HI (2nd)
Gaetz, Matt.	Fort Walton Beach, FL (1st)
Gallagher, Mike	Green Bay, WI (8th)
Gallego, Ruben	Phoenix, AZ (7th)
Garamendi, John	Walnut Grove, CA (3rd)
Garrett, Thomas A., Jr.	Scottsville, VA (5th)
Gianforte, Greg	Bozeman, MT (At Large)
Gibbs, Bob	Lakeville, OH (7th)
Gohmert, Louie	Tyler, TX (1st)
Gomez, Jimmy	Los Angeles, CA (34th)
Gonzalez, Vicente	McAllen, TX (15th)
Goodlatte, Bob.	Roanoke, VA (6th)
Gosar, Paul A.	Prescott, AZ (4th)
Gottheimer, Josh.	Wyckoff, NJ (5th)
Gowdy, Trey	Spartanburg, SC (4th)
Granger, Kay.	Fort Worth, TX (12th)
Graves, Garret	Baton Rouge, LA (6th)
Graves, Sam	Tarkio, MO (6th)
Graves, Tom	Ranger, GA (14th)
Green, Al.	Houston, TX (9th)
Green, Gene	Houston, TX (29th)
Griffith, H. Morgan	Salem, VA (9th)
Grijalva, Raúl M.	Tucson, AZ (3rd)
Grothman, Glenn	Glenbeulah, WI (6th)
Guthrie, Brett	Bowling Green, KY (2nd)
Gutiérrez, Luis V.	Chicago, IL (4th)
Hanabusa, Colleen	Honolulu, HI (1st)
Handel, Karen C.	Roswell, GA (6th)
Harper, Gregg	Pearl, MS (3rd)
Harris, Andy.	Cockeysville, MD (1st)
Hartzler, Vicky.	Harrisonville, MO (4th)
Hastings, Alcee L.	Delray Beach, FL (20th)
Heck, Denny	Olympia, WA (10th)

REPRESENTATIVES

Name	Home post office/Dist. no.
Hensarling, Jeb	Dallas, TX (5th)
Herrera Beutler, Jaime	Battle Ground, WA (3rd)
Hice, Jody B.	Monroe, GA (10th)
Higgins, Brian	Buffalo, NY (26th)
Higgins, Clay	Lafayette, LA (3rd)
Hill, J. French	Little Rock, AR (2nd)
Himes, James A.	Cos Cob, CT (4th)
Holding, George	Raleigh, NC (2nd)
Hollingsworth, Trey	Jeffersonville, IN (9th)
Hoyer, Steny H.	Mechanicsville, MD (5th)
Hudson, Richard	Concord, NC (8th)
Huffman, Jared	San Rafael, CA (2nd)
Huizenga, Bill	Zeeland, MI (2nd)
Hultgren, Randy	Plano, IL (14th)
Hunter, Duncan	Alpine, CA (50th)
Hurd, Will	San Antonio, TX (23rd)
Issa, Darrell E.	Vista, CA (49th)
Jackson Lee, Sheila	Houston, TX (18th)
Jayapal, Pramila	Seattle, WA (7th)
Jeffries, Hakeem S.	Brooklyn, NY (8th)
Jenkins, Evan H.	Huntington, WV (3rd)
Jenkins, Lynn	Topeka, KS (2nd)
Johnson, Bill	Marietta, OH (6th)
Johnson, Eddie Bernice	Dallas, TX (30th)
Johnson, Henry C. "Hank", Jr.	Lithonia, GA (4th)
Johnson, Mike	Benton, LA (4th)
Johnson, Sam	Plano, TX (3rd)
Jones, Walter B.	Farmville, NC (3rd)
Jordan, Jim	Urbana, OH (4th)
Joyce, David P.	Russell Township, OH (14th)
Kaptur, Marcy	Toledo, OH (9th)
Katko, John	Syracuse, NY (24th)
Keating, William R.	Bourne, MA (9th)
Kelly, Mike	Butler, PA (3rd)
Kelly, Robin L.	Matteson, IL (2nd)

Name	Home post office/Dist. no.
Kelly, Trent	Saltillo, MS (1st)
Kennedy, Joseph P. III	Newton, MA (4th)
Khanna, Ro	Fremont, CA (17th)
Kihuen, Ruben J.	Las Vegas, NV (4th)
Kildee, Daniel T.	Flushing, MI (5th)
Kilmer, Derek	Gig Harbor, WA (6th)
Kind, Ron	La Crosse, WI (3rd)
King, Peter T.	Seaford, NY (2nd)
King, Steve	Kiron, IA (4th)
Kinzinger, Adam	Channahon, IL (16th)
Knight, Stephen	Palmdale, CA (25th)
Krishnamoorthi, Raja	Schaumburg, IL (8th)
Kuster, Ann M.	Hopkinton, NH (2nd)
Kustoff, David	Germantown, TN (8th)
Labrador, Raúl R.	Eagle, ID (1st)
LaHood, Darin	Peoria, IL (18th)
LaMalfa, Doug	Oroville, CA (1st)
Lamborn, Doug	Colorado Springs, CO (5th)
Lance, Leonard	Clinton Township, NJ (7th)
Langevin, James R.	Warwick, RI (2nd)
Larsen, Rick	Everett, WA (2nd)
Larson, John B.	East Hartford, CT (1st)
Latta, Robert E.	Bowling Green, OH (5th)
Lawrence, Brenda L.	Southfield, MI (14th)
Lawson, Al, Jr.	Tallahassee, FL (5th)
Lee, Barbara	Oakland, CA (13th)
Levin, Sander M.	Royal Oak, MI (9th)
Lewis, Jason	Woodbury, MN (2nd)
Lewis, John	Atlanta, GA (5th)
Lieu, Ted	Torrance, CA (33rd)
Lipinski, Daniel	Western Springs, IL (3rd)
LoBiondo, Frank A.	Ventnor, NJ (2nd)
Loebsack, David	Iowa City, IA (2nd)
Lofgren, Zoe	San José, CA (19th)
Long, Billy	Springfield, MO (7th)

REPRESENTATIVES

Name	Home post office/Dist. no.
Loudermilk, Barry	Cassville, GA (11th)
Love, Mia B.	Saratoga Springs, UT (4th)
Lowenthal, Alan S.	Long Beach, CA (47th)
Lowey, Nita M.	Harrison, NY (17th)
Lucas, Frank D.	Cheyenne, OK (3rd)
Luetkemeyer, Blaine	St. Elizabeth, MO (3rd)
Luján, Ben Ray	Nambé, NM (3rd)
Lujan Grisham, Michelle	Albuquerque, NM (1st)
Lynch, Stephen F.	South Boston, MA (8th)
MacArthur, Thomas	Toms River, NJ (3rd)
Maloney, Carolyn B.	New York, NY (12th)
Maloney, Sean Patrick	Cold Spring, NY (18th)
Marchant, Kenny	Coppell, TX (24th)
Marino, Tom	Williamsport, PA (10th)
Marshall, Roger W.	Great Bend, KS (1st)
Massie, Thomas	Garrison, KY (4th)
Mast, Brian J.	Palm City, FL (18th)
Matsui, Doris O.	Sacramento, CA (6th)
McCarthy, Kevin	Bakersfield, CA (23rd)
McCaul, Michael T.	Austin, TX (10th)
McClintock, Tom	Roseville, CA (4th)
McCollum, Betty	St. Paul, MN (4th)
McEachin, A. Donald	Henrico, VA (4th)
McGovern, James P.	Worcester, MA (2nd)
McHenry, Patrick T.	Lake Norman, NC (10th)
McKinley, David B.	Wheeling, WV (1st)
McMorris Rodgers, Cathy	Spokane, WA (5th)
McNerney, Jerry	Stockton, CA (9th)
McSally, Martha	Tucson, AZ (2nd)
Meadows, Mark	Skyland, NC (11th)
Meehan, Patrick	Chadds Ford, PA (7th)
Meeks, Gregory W.	Queens, NY (5th)
Meng, Grace	Queens, NY (6th)
Messer, Luke	Greensburg, IN (6th)
Mitchell, Paul	Dryden, MI (10th)

Name	Home post office/Dist. no.
Moolenaar, John R.	Midland, MI (4th)
Mooney, Alexander X.	Charles Town, WV (2nd)
Moore, Gwen	Milwaukee, WI (4th)
Moulton, Seth	Salem, MA (6th)
Mullin, Markwayne	Westville, OK (2nd)
Murphy, Stephanie N.	Winter Park, FL (7th)
Nadler, Jerrold	New York, NY (10th)
Napolitano, Grace F.	Norwalk, CA (32nd)
Neal, Richard E.	Springfield, MA (1st)
Newhouse, Dan	Sunnyside, WA (4th)
Noem, Kristi L.	Castlewood, SD (At Large)
Nolan, Richard M.	Crosby, MN (8th)
Norcross, Donald	Camden City, NJ (1st)
Norman, Ralph	Rock Hill, SC (5th)
Nunes, Devin	Tulare, CA (22nd)
O'Halleran, Tom.	Sedona, AZ (1st)
Olson, Pete	Sugar Land, TX (22nd)
O'Rourke, Beto	El Paso, TX (16th)
Palazzo, Steven M.	Biloxi, MS (4th)
Pallone, Frank, Jr.	Long Branch, NJ (6th)
Palmer, Gary J.	Hoover, AL (6th)
Panetta, Jimmy	Carmel Valley, CA (20th)
Pascrell, Bill, Jr.	Paterson, NJ (9th)
Paulsen, Erik.	Eden Prairie, MN (3rd)
Payne, Donald M., Jr.	Newark, NJ (10th)
Pearce, Stevan	Hobbs, NM (2nd)
Pelosi, Nancy	San Francisco, CA (12th)
Perlmutter, Ed.	Golden, CO (7th)
Perry, Scott.	Dillsburg, PA (4th)
Peters, Scott H.	San Diego, CA (52nd)
Peterson, Collin C.	Detroit Lakes, MN (7th)
Pingree, Chellie	North Haven, ME (1st)
Pittenger, Robert.	Charlotte, NC (9th)
Pocan, Mark.	Madison, WI (2nd)
Poe, Ted	Atascocita, TX (2nd)

REPRESENTATIVES

Name	Home post office/Dist. no.
Poliquin, Bruce	Oakland, ME (2nd)
Polis, Jared.	Boulder, CO (2nd)
Posey, Bill	Rockledge, FL (8th)
Price, David E..	Chapel Hill, NC (4th)
Quigley, Mike	Chicago, IL (5th)
Raskin, Jamie	Takoma Park, MD (8th)
Ratcliffe, John	Heath, TX (4th)
Reed, Tom	Corning, NY (23rd)
Reichert, David G.	Auburn, WA (8th)
Renacci, James B.	Wadsworth, OH (16th)
Rice, Kathleen M.	Garden City, NY (4th)
Rice, Tom	Myrtle Beach, SC (7th)
Richmond, Cedric L..	New Orleans, LA (2nd)
Roby, Martha	Montgomery, AL (2nd)
Roe, David P..	Johnson City, TN (1st)
Rogers, Harold.	Somerset, KY (5th)
Rogers, Mike	Anniston, AL (3rd)
Rohrabacher, Dana	Costa Mesa, CA (48th)
Rokita, Todd	Brownsburg, IN (4th)
Rooney, Francis	Naples, FL (19th)
Rooney, Thomas J..	Okeechobee, FL (17th)
Rosen, Jacky	Henderson, NV (3rd)
Roskam, Peter J.	Wheaton, IL (6th)
Ros-Lehtinen, Ileana	Miami, FL (27th)
Ross, Dennis A.	Lakeland, FL (15th)
Rothfus, Keith J.	Sewickley, PA (12th)
Rouzer, David	McGee's Crossroad, NC (7th)
Roybal-Allard, Lucille.	Downey, CA (40th)
Royce, Edward R.	Fullerton, CA (39th)
Ruiz, Raul	Coachella, CA (36th)
Ruppersberger, C.A. Dutch	Cockeysville, MD (2nd)
Rush, Bobby L.	Chicago, IL (1st)
Russell, Steve.	Oklahoma City, OK (5th)
Rutherford, John H..	Jacksonville, FL (4th)
Ryan, Paul D.	Janesville, WI (1st)

Name	*Home post office/Dist. no.*
Ryan, Tim	Warren, OH (13th)
Sánchez, Linda T.	Whittier, CA (38th)
Sanford, Mark	Charleston, SC (1st)
Sarbanes, John P.	Baltimore, MD (3rd)
Scalise, Steve	Jefferson, LA (1st)
Schakowsky, Janice D.	Evanston, IL (9th)
Schiff, Adam B.	Burbank, CA (28th)
Schneider, Bradley Scott.	Deerfield, IL (10th)
Schrader, Kurt.	Canby, OR (5th)
Schweikert, David	Fountain Hills, AZ (6th)
Scott, Austin	Tifton, GA (8th)
Scott, David	Atlanta, GA (13th)
Scott, Robert C. "Bobby"	Newport News, VA (3rd)
Sensenbrenner, F. James, Jr.	Menomonee Falls, WI (5th)
Serrano, José E.	Bronx, NY (15th)
Sessions, Pete	Dallas, TX (32nd)
Sewell, Terri A.	Birmingham, AL (7th)
Shea-Porter, Carol.	Rochester, NH (1st)
Sherman, Brad	Sherman Oaks, CA (30th)
Shimkus, John	Collinsville, IL (15th)
Shuster, Bill	Hollidaysburg, PA (9th)
Simpson, Michael K.	Idaho Falls, ID (2nd)
Sinema, Kyrsten	Phoenix, AZ (9th)
Sires, Albio.	West New York, NJ (8th)
Slaughter, Louise McIntosh	Fairport, NY (25th)
Smith, Adam.	Bellevue, WA (9th)
Smith, Adrian	Gering, NE (3rd)
Smith, Christopher H.	Hamilton, NJ (4th)
Smith, Jason	Salem, MO (8th)
Smith, Lamar	San Antonio, TX (21st)
Smucker, Lloyd	Lancaster, PA (16th)
Soto, Darren	Kissimmee, FL (9th)
Speier, Jackie.	Hillsborough, CA (14th)
Stefanik, Elise M.	Willsboro, NY (21st)
Stewart, Chris	Farmington, UT (2nd)

REPRESENTATIVES

Name	Home post office/Dist. no.
Stivers, Steve	Columbus, OH (15th)
Suozzi, Thomas R.	Glen Cove, NY (3rd)
Swalwell, Eric	Pleasanton, CA (15th)
Takano, Mark	Riverside, CA (41st)
Taylor, Scott	Virginia Beach, VA (2nd)
Tenney, Claudia	New Hartford, NY (22nd)
Thompson, Bennie G.	Bolton, MS (2nd)
Thompson, Glenn	Howard, PA (5th)
Thompson, Mike.	St. Helena, CA (5th)
Thornberry, Mac	Clarendon, TX (13th)
Tipton, Scott R.	Cortez, CO (3rd)
Titus, Dina.	Las Vegas, NV (1st)
Tonko, Paul	Amsterdam, NY (20th)
Torres, Norma J.	Pomona, CA (35th)
Trott, David A.	Birmingham, MI (11th)
Tsongas, Niki	Lowell, MA (3rd)
Turner, Michael R.	Dayton, OH (10th)
Upton, Fred	St. Joseph, MI (6th)
Valadao, David G.	Hanford, CA (21st)
Vargas, Juan.	San Diego, CA (51st)
Veasey, Marc A.	Fort Worth, TX (33rd)
Vela, Filemon	Brownsville, TX (34th)
Velázquez, Nydia M.	Brooklyn, NY (7th)
Visclosky, Peter J.	Merrillville, IN (1st)
Wagner, Ann.	Ballwin, MO (2nd)
Walberg, Tim	Tipton, MI (7th)
Walden, Greg	Hood River, OR (2nd)
Walker, Mark	Greensboro, NC (6th)
Walorski, Jackie	Elkhart, IN (2nd)
Walters, Mimi	Irvine, CA (45th)
Walz, Timothy J.	Mankato, MN (1st)
Wasserman Schultz, Debbie	Weston, FL (23rd)
Waters, Maxine	Los Angeles, CA (43rd)
Watson Coleman, Bonnie	Ewing Township, NJ (12th)
Weber, Randy K., Sr.	Friendswood, TX (14th)

Name	Home post office/Dist. no.
Webster, Daniel	Clermont, FL (11th)
Welch, Peter	Norwich, VT (At Large)
Wenstrup, Brad R.	Cincinnati, OH (2nd)
Westerman, Bruce	Hot Springs, AR (4th)
Williams, Roger	Austin, TX (25th)
Wilson, Frederica S.	Miami Gardens, FL (24th)
Wilson, Joe	Springdale, SC (2nd)
Wittman, Robert J.	Montross, VA (1st)
Womack, Steve	Rogers, AR (3rd)
Woodall, Rob	Lawrenceville, GA (7th)
Yarmuth, John A.	Louisville, KY (3rd)
Yoder, Kevin	Overland Park, KS (3rd)
Yoho, Ted S.	Gainesville, FL (3rd)
Young, David	Van Meter, IA (3rd)
Young, Don	Fort Yukon, AK (At Large)
Zeldin, Lee M.	Shirley, NY (1st)

REPRESENTATIVES

DELEGATES

Name	Home post office
Bordallo, Madeleine Z.	Hagatna, GU
Norton, Eleanor Holmes	District of Columbia
Plaskett, Stacey E.	St. Croix, VI
Radewagen, Aumua Amata Coleman.	Pago Pago, AS
Sablan, Gregorio Kilili Camacho	Saipan, MP

RESIDENT COMMISSIONER

Name	Home post office
González-Colón, Jenniffer.	San Juan, PR